Back Garden Seed Saving
Keeping our vegetable heritage alive

Back Garden
Seed saving

Keeping our vegetable heritage alive

by Sue Stickland

Illustrations by Sue Kendall

First published in 2001 by eco-logic books

Copyright © HDRA – The Organic Organisation 2001
Illustrations © Sue Kendall 2001

ISBN 1 899233 09 1

Illustrations by Sue Kendall
Photography by Sue Stickland
Design & Typesetting by HMD 0117 914 5536
Printed & Bound in the UK by Russell Press
Additional Photography by: Audrey Adcock, Peter Anderson, Diane Bailey, The Beanstalk Project, Tony Dunn, Eddie Lancaster, Toni Nice, Philip Rainford and Don Vincent.

Further copies of the book can be purchased from:
eco-logic books
10-12 Picton Street
Bristol BS6 5QA
England

Telephone: 0117 942 0165
Fax: 0117 942 0164
Email: books@eco-logic.demon.co.uk

eco-logic books produce a mail order catalogue of books that promote practical solutions to environmental problems, organic gardening, sustainable development, permaculture and related topics. For a FREE copy of this catalogue contact them at the above address.

Contents

Back Garden Seed Saving ~ Keeping our vegetable heritage alive

Foreword

by Thelma Barlow

I've been a keen gardener for many years. In fact, I'm an organic gardener, because I believe that we ought to look after our own little piece of the planet in an environmentally sensitive way. That's why I value genetic diversity. There are countless thousands of different varieties of plants out there and as far as I am concerned they are all important. Who knows what genetic information they contain that might benefit future generations. And they give us so much pleasure too. All those wonderful shapes and colours and fragrances and tastes. Their history, also, makes for really interesting reading. Who wouldn't want to know the story behind The Lazy Housewife french bean for instance?

As you can see from Sue's book there are many other old vegetable varieties with a tantalising tale to tell. In some cases they survived because one gardener took a liking to them and grew them year after year. Sometimes they are intertwined with people who had sad stories of hunger and poverty. All the seeds that come down to us are the legacy of previous generations for whom these varieties really mattered and we too should value them, not only for their own merits or to maintain a rich diversity of vegetables but to honour those who bequeathed them to us.

Our ancestors saved seeds to survive; seed saving was part of the annual cycle of producing food. They had no garden centres or glossy catalogues to choose from and early gardening books probably all gave advice on how to save seed. Now it is such a rare practice that it is seldom mentioned, except in special books like this. Here you will find some practical advice gleaned from people who do it year after year. And if, unlike me, you can't do it yourself, just enjoy the stories of the hidden treasures and much-loved heirlooms revealed in these pages.

Introduction

It is August, and on his smallholding in the Derbyshire hills Frank Clark is harvesting broad beans. The green ones for eating have long been picked, but these are dried pods – the lower ones on selected plants that he has carefully earmarked for seed. Frank's father used to grow the same broad bean, and he in turn had inherited the seed from his father, so this strain of the crop has been growing here in Derbyshire for more than a century. It is reliable, always germinating and setting well even in the harsh upland climate, and it yields as many tasty beans as any modern variety he has seen, so Frank sees no reason to change. He and his brother Richard call it 'Clark's Classic'.

In this way, gardeners have kept hundreds of old and unusual vegetable varieties in cultivation. Some are family heirlooms like the Clark's broad bean; some are commercial varieties no longer available in the seed catalogues; some are local strains of crops. They are precious to the gardeners that save them, both as reminders of people and places, and for the way they grow and how they taste. However, they also have wider value, providing a peephole into horticultural history and a reserve of genetic diversity. They could have unique qualities – disease resistance or drought tolerance, perhaps – vital to crops in the future.

The Heritage Seed Library run by HDRA, the Organic Organisation, aims to conserve such otherwise unobtainable vegetable varieties and make them available to gardeners. It began as a small collection in the 1970s, brought together by HDRA's founder the late Lawrence Hills. He realised that varieties were being lost through the restricting effect of EC legislation and saw a seed 'library' as one way of saving them. By 1999 the Heritage Seed Library contained around 30 vegetable types and 700 varieties or cultivars, and was distributing around 42,000 packets of seed. Its members are also encouraged to save seed for themselves, thus varieties in the collection are grown in all sorts of conditions by gardeners throughout the country, and not just kept in cold storage.

But what about varieties not in the Seed Library, still being grown by just one elderly gardener, for example, or a group of allotment holders whose site is under threat? They could easily be lost for ever. Seed saving is no longer the integral part of vegetable growing that it once was. It is rarely mentioned in gardening books or television programmes, and today's gardeners are under much more pressure to buy the newest popular varieties, temptingly displayed in glossy packets, and sold cheaply in garden centres and even in supermarkets.

It was to draw in such endangered varieties, and to encourage the art of home seed saving, that in 1998 HDRA's Seed Search was launched, with support from the Department of the Environment, Transport and the Regions. Publicity through local and national papers, radio and television, gardening magazines and flower shows, appealed to gardeners to send in seed of home-saved varieties. With the help of volunteers in their own gardens, the varieties were grown on, their performance and characteristics recorded, and more seed was saved. The project was something of a gamble – nobody really knew how many varieties were being kept by gardeners, and still less whether any of them would be really different.

However, the steady response to the appeal showed without doubt that, despite the lure of the new and the glossy, many gardeners were still saving seed for themselves. It didn't matter whether they had tiny gardens, allotments or smallholdings, or in what part of the country they lived. The majority of the gardeners were elderly, however: a good proportion of them over the age of 70. Some had younger family members interested in gardening to whom they could pass on seeds but many did not. A strain of large black-seeded runner bean, for example, was sent anonymously to the Seed Search with a note saying that the seeds were known locally as 'Coal beans', grown by miners in the Shropshire village of St Martins for generations and passed down through their families. 'Sadly very few are left who grow them now,' the note continued 'I was given these by an old gentleman who can no longer garden so I am sending them to you'.

Outside the family, it became clear that allotments are fertile places for sharing tales and passing on seeds of the 'Allotment bean' or the 'local shallot', for example. In a few places, such as Bath, this informal swapping has developed into an organised local seed saving group, with regular meetings and 'seed swap' evenings. In other areas, schools and community groups are using seed saving as a way of introducing young people to organic gardening, biodiversity, or local history – or a combination of all three.

As well as drawing in an abundance of reliable home-saved varieties with long pedigrees, the Seed Search brought forth a few exciting discoveries, together with some tantalising glimpses of history and many heart-warming stories of gardeners past. There was the exceptionally large black-eyed pea that could not be matched even by the large pea collection at the John Innes Centre in Norwich, for example, and the pea that Lord Carnarvon claimed to have found in Tutankhamun's tomb. Then there was the French bean that was said to have been washed up by a shipwreck, and the kale that was taken by emigrants to Canada in the mid nineteenth century and returned to this country 150 years later.

Whatever the benefits of modern hybrids, it seems that old varieties still have much to offer gardeners. The latest strains of runner beans may give long stringless pods, but will they crop well on a cold windswept site? No seed company tests for this. Dwarf peas may be the easiest to grow commercially, but you will still find the six foot types in many gardens – they look attractive, crop for longer and taste 'like peas used to taste before the freezer'. As such varieties have disappeared from the seed catalogues over the past few decades, gardeners have kept them in cultivation.

The process is still going on: old and unusual varieties for which the seed companies find there is little demand are in constant threat of being dropped. However, you don't have to let a few large seed companies determine what you grow – you can seek out old and unusual varieties from the Heritage Seed Library and other seed saving groups, or from specialist catalogues, or from other gardeners, and you can save seed for yourself. Seed saving can be very easy and immensely satisfying. Just the sight of onion or carrot flowerheads humming with bees, for example, or the scent of beetroot in full bloom adds a new dimension to gardening, and at the end you will have seed from your own crops to sow next year, and extra to give away to friends and neighbours. What is more, growing old and unusual varieties means that you really can make a contribution to 'biodiversity' – a concept easy to approve in theory, but more difficult to help in practice.

In this book you can find out about some of the vegetable varieties never – or no longer – found in the seed catalogues, and others that are there now but may not be for much longer. It introduces you to some of the gardeners who grow such varieties, their tales and tips, and their infectious enthusiasm. Most important, it gives easy to follow crop-by-crop guidelines to help you save seed for yourself.

Rebecca Latter with home saved variety of the tall pea Simpsons Special.

Where do all the seeds come from?

A cold winter's day, a cosy armchair, and a clutch of coloured seed catalogues – this is how most of us choose the seeds for our vegetable plots next year. We rarely ask ourselves where they came from, and it can come as a surprise to learn that, with very few exceptions, most of the seeds will have been grown abroad. Many of the new varieties will also have been bred overseas, and will almost certainly be intended to meet the demands of commercial growers and not necessarily those of gardeners. Our influence on the final content of the seed packets that we open with such anticipation in spring is very small. However, this was not always the case.

The early seed trade

In the 14th and 15th centuries, seeds were not something most ordinary folk would be able to buy easily or to afford. They probably grew a lot themselves, both to sow and to exchange with other gardeners. However, merchants in London and other major ports did import seeds, others came from the surpluses of monastery gardens, and in the large towns these seeds were sold by some grocers and general shopkeepers. However, for them seeds were just a sideline – there would not usually have been a large range or any organised list of what was on offer. In the country people could buy seeds at fairs and markets, or from travelling pedlars, but there was unlikely to be a reliable supply.

Unlike gardening books today, one of the earliest handbooks for gardeners *The Feat of Gardening* compiled by Master John Gardener at the end of the 14th century gives very practical instructions for saving seed. He advises, for example, that onion seed will show black when ripe and should be ready at Lammas (August 1st) if the onions were set or sown in March or April – exactly the sort of tip that is useful to would-be seedsavers. In 1573, farmer Thomas Tusser wrote, in verse, and had printed *A Hundred Good Pointes of Husbandrie*, which also encouraged ordinary country folk to save seeds:

> 'Good huswifes in sommer will save their own seedes,
> Against the next yeere, as occasion needes.
> One seede for another, to make an exchange,
> With fellowlie neighbourhood seemeth not strange.'

It was the development of market gardening to supply the ever-growing population of London that led to a more organised production of vegetable seeds. Much of the initiative and expertise probably came from Dutch immigrants who arrived in the middle of the 16th century to settle in southern and eastern England: they first produced vegetables for sale and then in some areas, particularly round Sandwich in Kent and Colchester in Essex began to specialise in seeds. Many seeds would still have been imported, but a significant aspect of this home production was that, as these knowledgeable gardeners selected the best plants from their crops and grew them on for seed, many well adapted local strains were developed: Sandwich beans and Sandwich radishes, for example, were on sale by the 1670s. The Vale of Evesham also developed both as a market gardening and seed production area, and by the end of the 17th century was exporting seeds through the port of Gloucester to other parts of the country.

At the same time, the first specialist seedsmen began trading in London. One of the earliest surviving seed lists is that of William Lucas, who in around 1677 had a shop 'at the sign of the Naked Boy' near Strand Bridge. It includes seeds of a wide range of different vegetables and often several basic types of each, so there are three kinds of carrots (Orange, Yellow, Red), three kinds of turnip (Long, Round, Yellow) and five kinds of onions (Strasburgh [sic], Red Spanish, White Spanish, French,

English). These early seedsmen sold seeds by weight, and there were no prices on their lists. The customers were probably mainly market gardeners, or gardeners to country gentlemen or to the richer inhabitants of London. In the 18th century, the number of specialist seedsmen in London increased considerably and they also began to set up in provincial towns. In 1764, for example, John Harrison from Leicester bought himself out of the navy and set up a shop in the city – the beginnings of the local seed firm Harrison & Son which traded for over 200 years. Seed catalogues also became more sophisticated, now showing prices, and with an increasing range of crops and varieties.

The Victorian era

The vast growth of the towns and cities in the 19th century meant a corresponding increase in market gardens and gardeners to supply them, and many of these selected their own special strains of crops and saved their own seed. The best of these local strains were taken up by the seed companies and made more widely available: '...scarcely any other is grown in the market gardens around Cheltenham' said the *Gardeners' Chronicle* in 1889, praising the Cheltenham Green Top beetroot, which is still sold today. Similarly, the head gardeners on the large country estates were also selecting for earlier or more productive plants, or bigger or tastier fruit. A variety carrying the name of the estate, which won prizes at shows and was then widely sold, could bring considerable prestige. There are numerous examples in Victorian catalogues and a few are still familiar: the Blenheim Orange melon bred on the Duke of Marlborough's estate at Blenheim, for example, and the Rousham Park Hero onion bred on the Oxfordshire estate of that name.

Most of the varieties in catalogues were thus developed by market gardeners, or by country gentlemen or their gardeners, using a combination of intuition and experience coupled with keen observation. A few were the result of deliberate hybridisation – the wrinkle-seeded peas produced by Thomas Knight, for example, who was one of the earliest systematic plant breeders – but there was no knowledge of the laws of genetics.

Many of the familiar seed company names became established in the early 1800s: James Carter first set up his small bow-windowed shop in High Holborn, for example, and Sutton & Sons sent out their first illustrated and priced catalogue at this time. Later in the century, seed catalogues became even more elaborate, giving detailed cultivation instructions, gardening calendars and reflective articles often written in rather pompous prose: '...this generation's work in the Vegetable Garden has accomplished much substantial improvement in the means and way of life, and has caused corresponding progress in the acquisition and advancement of the higher kinds of knowledge' said Sutton's *Spring Catalogue and Amateur's Guide* in 1881.

The number of varieties of each vegetable crop on offer was almost bewildering: the same Sutton's catalogue listed over 25 varieties just of frame cucumbers, for example, and printed many glowing testimonials of them from satisfied customers. Although these came from a wider range of occupations and social classes rather than the wealthy customers of the 18th century seed firms, seeds were still beyond the means of many. In 1863 Sutton's offered seeds at a discount, or possibly even free, to '...Clergymen and others who desire to encourage their Cottagers in the cultivation of their gardens.'

Synonyms and seed quality

The Victorian catalogues may have listed hundreds of differently named varieties, but not all of them were distinct. It was common practice for seed companies to take a variety that another company had produced, and simply rename and sell it under their own name. Sometimes one company was accused of selling the same variety under two, or even three, different names. 'To be able to secure pure stocks of long-tried standard vegetables is not easy for the public while the seedsman affixes a new name and the name of his house to almost everything he sells,' proclaimed the well respected gardener and author William Robinson. He was writing in the preface to the English edition of *The Vegetable Garden*, a book based on the experience of senior members of the Vilmorin family who were owners of the oldest and largest seed company in France – a country where, says Mr Robinson, this practice is almost unknown. The book is unique in the range of crops and varieties it covers and in the detail in which it describes their characteristics, and William Robinson's additional notes for English growers give a valuable view of the horticultural scene at the time.

As well as the confusion over names, another problem was seed quality. It was perhaps not surprising that the early pedlars who wandered the countryside would sell dud seeds: carrot seeds that were too old to germinate, for example, or cheap turnip seed substituted for a more exotic (and expensive) brassica. After all, the buyer would not discover the fraud until long after he had gone. However, such practices were also rife amongst seed merchants in the 1800s, and this was another good reason for gardeners to save their own seeds. In 1829 William Cobbett in his book the *English Gardener* warns that '...the eye is no guide at all' when it comes to buying seed and, for each vegetable that the book covers, describes how gardeners can save their own.

In 1866, a commission into seed quality reported that merchants kept seed too long – sometimes dyeing it to improve its appearance, or adding contaminants such as dead seeds or sand, and as a result legislation was passed in 1869 making the adulteration of seeds illegal. However, little provision was made for its enforcement.

Professional plant breeding

The first few decades of the twentieth century brought many changes. The austerity of war and the years of depression swept away the diversity of the Victorian and Edwardian kitchen gardens. There were not the men to tend them nor money to pay for their upkeep. Increasingly vegetables were grown on a field scale instead of in small market gardens. As part of the quest for efficient agricultural production, at least the problems of seed quality were finally addressed. Emergency regulations on seed testing were made during the 1914-18 war, and were eventually replaced in 1922 by permanent legislation: the Seeds Regulations 1922 which required seeds to be tested and meet minimum standards of germination.

With the recognition of the work of the 19th century Moravian monk Gregor Mendel, who had worked out the natural rules of genetic inheritance, plant breeding became more of a science. The professional plant breeders now looking for crops to suit the changed social and agricultural conditions often made deliberate crosses of likely parent plants, before selecting and growing on the progeny to produce new open-pollinated varieties. However, at that time commercial growers did not use large amounts of chemicals or sophisticated machinery, and most produce was sold fresh at local shops and markets, which needed a continual supply of a wide range of crops. Their requirements were thus not that different to those of gardeners, and many of the vegetable varieties that were bred during this period became valuable garden favourites: the tomato Ailsa Craig, the broad bean Red Epicure and the runner bean Kelvedon Marvel, for example.

There were many small family based seed firms: experienced seedsmen employing technical staff on their own trial grounds. Each had its own seed list which often included the company's special selections and sometimes local varieties. Some of their vegetable seeds were grown in England, mainly in Essex, and growing seeds under contract could be a profitable sideline for farmers. A few farmers and some of the remaining market gardeners also continued to save seed for themselves. In the Vale of Evesham, for example, where even neighbouring villages sometimes had their own distinct strains of Brussels sprout. Nevertheless, it became increasingly more economic for seed merchants to buy seeds from abroad. As one contemporary gardening writer put it: '...No-one cared where they [the seeds] came from, or how and when they were grown...Britain paid her way, sailed her ships, and imported her seeds'.

Saving seeds for victory

Wartime blockades prevented all that, however, and by 1942 seeds were becoming scarce. Increased production at home was imperative. With the support of the Ministry of Agriculture, substantial acreages in many counties were put down to growing seeds, and glasshouses that in pre-war days grew quantities of cut flowers were now filled with the less attractive aroma of drying onion heads.

Mr Honey, a Heritage Seed Library member who worked for a London seed merchant in 1943, can remember that in the summer months he was sent out to 'rogue' various crops being grown for seed: 'Evesham Special sprouts and Myatts Offenham cabbage in Bedfordshire, January King cabbage and Ormskirk savoy in Essex, various tomatoes in the Chichester area...leeks in Surrey'. As seeds were now being grown by those with little or no experience, problems with cross-pollination inevitably arose and zoning schemes were introduced in some counties, whereby only certain crops and varieties were permitted in any one zone.

As part of the Dig for Victory campaign, the Ministry of Agriculture also encouraged gardeners to save their own seeds, and as varieties received by the Seed Search project indicate, some gardeners did not stop in 1945 but have carried on doing this ever since. Two of the varieties sent in – a broad bean and a runner bean – were originally from seed issued to allotment holders that had been donated by American benefactors as part of the War Relief effort.

Modern farming and marketing

The seed industry received little support after 1945, however, and soon the whole system of farming and marketing began to change dramatically. We started to buy more processed vegetables and less in-season fresh produce, and the supermarkets began to take over the role of greengrocers. Farming became more mechanised and used more chemicals and, to satisfy the new markets, farmers grew larger acreages of a much narrower range of crops. Supermarkets were not interested in local produce – they wanted large amounts of a single crop on the same day so that it could go to a central packing house and then out to all their branches. They also wanted produce that was uniform in shape and size for mechanical packing and easy pricing, and it had to be robust enough to withstand the travelling and life on the supermarket shelf.

These were the qualities that plant breeders were now aiming for in new vegetable varieties, and any variety that possessed them would be likely to sell in large quantities to commercial growers. There was much less incentive for seed companies to keep supplying those varieties that were bought in small quantities only by gardeners, and certainly no profit in breeding varieties for amateur growers. In fact, plant breeding had become even more sophisticated and expensive, often using laboratory techniques and specialised equipment. For an increasing number of crops, the new varieties emerging were F1 hybrids, the seeds of which must always be produced by crossing two separate inbred parent lines. These F1 varieties gave the uniformity that the commercial growers and the supermarkets required and, since any seed collected from them did not produce plants that were true-to-type, the commercial interests of the seed company were well protected. The new varieties often appeared in gardening catalogues as 'good for freezing', which simply meant that they all had to be harvested at once.

It was only the large companies with a variety of outlets that could afford the trained staff and facilities now necessary in the seed industry. Smaller firms without the same resources could not compete. Many closed down, others amalgamated into larger companies, and some of these themselves were taken over by multinationals whose main interests were often in other fields such as oil or chemicals. In 1976, Lawrence Hills wrote from HDRA to all the seed company addresses he could find. The reply from R. A. Morris Ltd in Birmingham was typical:

'I regret I cannot meet your request for a seed catalogue for I am closing down the business in a week or two. The present day rates and rents are more than a business like mine, which is of a seasonal nature and a small unit of sale can meet'.

Even larger companies were having similar problems. Carters, for example, was absorbed into Cuthberts in 1966 and, in the mid 1970s, Cuthberts together with Dobies, was taken over by a large Swedish conglomerate. Harrisons of Leicester joined with three other family businesses in 1962 to form ASMER seeds which was the UK's largest privately owned seed company, before this too closed in 1993. Every time a small firm closed or was taken over, its seed list simply disappeared or was rationalised, and some varieties were lost.

The seed which the remaining companies trialled and packaged for sale was by now almost all produced abroad. In 1959, for example, 600 hectares in Essex were under cultivation for runner bean seeds alone. In 1970, the total land devoted to all flower and vegetable seed in the county was only 800 hectares and by 1985 this had dropped to barely 200 hectares. Today, Kings Seeds of Coggeshall in Essex is one of the few companies to grow any range of vegetable seeds in the UK.

Illegal varieties

The final threat to the survival of old vegetable varieties came in the form of EU legislation. In 1964, the Plant Varieties and Seeds Act proposed that all vegetable varieties offered for sale must be registered on a UK 'National List', with seed companies invited to submit varieties for inclusion. When the UK entered the European Union in 1973, this legislation came into force, and it then became an offence punishable by a fine (then £400, now very much more) to market a variety that was neither on the UK List nor on that of one of the other member states. The aim behind the legislation was to protect consumers by ensuring that seeds actually delivered what was promised on the seed packet. Unfortunately, it also had the effect of accelerating the loss of old vegetable varieties and of severely limiting the choice of gardeners.

Many varieties were never included on the list in the first place – those not submitted by the seed companies for trial or, for one reason or another, not commercially available at the time. Then there was the problem of determining which varieties were true synonyms. This became particularly evident when the National Lists of all the EU member states were amalgamated into a single 'Common Catalogue'. Inevitably some varieties must have been marketed under different names in different countries, but by 1980 a total of 1,547 varieties had been deleted and it was said by campaigning organisations at the time that only 591 of these were true synonyms. As Lawrence Hills pointed out, all too often the judgement was made on external appearance so, for example, 'the onion Up-to-Date, the strongest yet, became officially the same as the mild Bedfordshire Champion', even though Up-to-Date had been shown in previous trials to have good disease resistance while that of Bedfordshire Champion was below average.

Once the National List was established, it became extremely expensive to add varieties or to reinstate any that had been deleted, and this is still the case. If a seed company wants to register a variety, it has to submit it for trial by the Plant Variety Rights Office (PVRO) to make sure that it is Distinct from other varieties, that all the plants are Uniform, and that the variety is Stable from generation to generation. This 'DUS' test now costs around £2000, which is a lot to pay if the variety is only going to be sold in small quantities to gardeners, and some of the old varieties are anyway too variable to pass the uniformity test. If a variety is accepted onto the list, the seed company that submitted it becomes the official 'maintainer' of the variety and has to pay an annual fee to keep it there. It also has to send samples of seed to the PVRO when requested.

In addition to National Listing, the 1964 Plant Varieties and Seeds Act introduced the idea of Plant Variety Rights (PVR). This enabled breeders of some new varieties to receive a royalty from anyone who multiplied them in order to sell the seed. PVR rightly rewards the breeders for work they have done in producing a new variety that is eligible for PVR, although it can help make these varieties even more profitable for a seed company compared with the old garden favourites.

Saving old varieties

It was to get around the law on marketing unlisted varieties that Lawrence Hills proposed the idea of a 'Seed Library' for HDRA members. Those who sent a contribution towards postage and handling would be 'given' seeds, and in turn would save their own seeds and return some to the Library. The operative word in the legislation is 'marketing' not selling, and one company had actually been prevented from giving away free seeds of an unlisted radish variety. However, even if the Seed Library went against the spirit of the law, MAFF chose to ignore it and it continued to flourish. In 1992 it became the Heritage Seed Library, run as it is today, with a separate membership, yearly catalogue, and volunteer Seed Guardians to help maintain the collection.

Lawrence Hills recognised that the loss of old varieties did more than just affect gardeners – it endangered the security of our future food supplies: 'The future may well need seeds having pollution tolerance as well as disease resistance' he said 'and we cannot afford to allow the destruction of valuable genetic material in the interests of commercial or bureaucratic tidiness'. In 1975 he launched a campaign to start a 'Seed Bank' for long term storage of seeds, so that the genetic diversity found in old vegetable varieties would be available to plant breeders in years to come. The government was reluctant to fund such a scheme, but eventually the charity Oxfam provided the resources to set up a national Vegetable Gene Bank at what is now Horticultural Research International (HRI) at Wellesbourne in Warwickshire.

Back in the market place, some seed companies avoided prosecution under the new National Listing laws by selling plants – or even chitted seeds – of unlisted varieties, as these are not covered by the regulations. Limited quantities of unlisted varieties can also be marketed for trial purposes, so others asked customers to report on those that they sold. However, the law still placed great limitations on small specialist seed companies wanting to sell old or local varieties, and on the choice available to gardeners.

Signs of change

In 1997 came slight signs of change, or at least there was official talk about it. The European Parliament recognised the threat that the seed laws posed to genetic conservation and proposed that under 'specific conditions' to be established there might be 'growing and marketing of landraces and varieties which are naturally adapted to the local and regional conditions'. However, there was – and still is – much bureaucracy to overcome. In the autumn of 2000 there are proposed new regulations in the UK, not yet passed by parliament, under which old varieties could remain on the list without a maintainer, and hence could still be legally sold – a step in the right direction, although rather little, rather late.

With the relaxation of official pressure and increased interest from gardeners, seed companies are selling more and more old and unusual vegetable varieties. There are small companies that specialise in 'heritage' varieties, and others that specialise in selling every conceivable variety of a particular crop, such as tomatoes or peppers for example. Even many of the larger companies are selling 'heritage collections' of seeds. However, there are many varieties – the family heirlooms and local strains of crops – that the companies will never sell. Even old commercial varieties, sold in small quantities with seeds sourced from abroad, are not secure. The only way to ensure that you will always be able to grow them is to save seed for yourself.

Why save your own?

As the previous history indicates, the gulf between gardeners and plant breeders has never been wider, and most gardeners see vegetable seed as something that comes ready grown and safely packeted. Yet saving seed is as much part of the cycle of growing your own food as sowing, planting and harvesting, and need be no more difficult. As HDRA's Seed Search has shown, there are many good reasons why some continue to save seed for themselves.

Garden varieties

The fact that traditional varieties have been ousted from the seed catalogues has been a strong incentive for many gardeners to start saving seeds. These varieties still have a lot to offer, and the new varieties bred for commercial markets do not always suit gardener's needs. Commercially produced tomatoes, for example, have to have skins tough enough to withstand mechanical handling and a lot of travelling, whereas gardeners – and cooks – prefer thin-skinned fruit that do not need peeling. Appearance doesn't matter either, as long as it has a good flavour. When Eric Skinn from Rotherham found that Carters had stopped selling his favourite Carters Fruit tomato he rang up to ask them why:

> 'Their answer was that the housewife only wants round, medium-sized tomatoes! Carters Fruit gets big and is positively ugly to look at, but it tastes beautiful – that's what is important.'

Luckily Mr Skinn managed to obtain some seed of Carters Fruit from another gardener and has now been saving his own for over 25 years.

Something different

The new varieties also give a limited choice. There may appear to be lots in the catalogue, but they are often very similar to one another – reflecting the colour of fruit or the size of root that is acceptable for market, rather than the range that the crop actually has to offer.

The supermarkets might only want round red tomatoes, for example, but in heritage collections – and home-saved in gardens and on allotments – you will find ones that are white, or purple, or still green when ripe, and ones that come in all sorts of shapes and sizes. For example Mr Bull from Staines sent a remarkable long pointed tomato to the Seed Search, which a neighbouring allotment holder had been growing and saving for years.

It is not only appearance that matters. Unlike modern plant breeders, gardeners are always looking to extend the range and flexibility of their crops. They may want to harvest at a different stage to the norm – to pick the young whole pods of broad beans, for example – or to eat produce raw when it is normally cooked. They may want to eat different parts of the plants – the green seed pods of radishes instead of the roots, the flowers of squashes, the leaves of beetroot, or the stems of calabrese – parts that would never be commercially harvested and that plant breeders may even be trying to reduce. Old varieties with more variability, grown before the days of mechanisation and mass markets, are far more likely to satisfy these needs. French beans used for fresh-shelled or dried beans, rather than the green pod, are one of the best examples. There are a myriad of old commercial and home-saved varieties successfully grown by UK gardeners, even though there are few in the seed catalogues bred for drying, and in this country they are not a commercial crop.

Bulls Blood

Although gardeners do not have labour cost or profit margins to watch, they do have other constraints, and one of these is often lack of space. Thus varieties that look good in a flower bed or potager are particularly valuable – the old violet-flagged leek Bleu de Solaise, for example, or the beetroot Bull's Blood that was used as a bedding plant in Victorian times. This is often why gardeners have kept old tall peas in cultivation, and over a dozen different varieties were collected by the Seed Search project even though hardly any now remain on the National List. Their height makes it impractical to grow and harvest them commercially, but in a garden they can give a good yield in a small space. They will also crop over a longer period than dwarf varieties, and can be used as a feature – over an arch or up a decorative screen. Some have attractive bicoloured flowers: the old catalogue variety Carouby de Maussane or the heirloom variety Eat All, for example.

One tall pea sent to the Seed Search by Mr Bound from Hampshire was strikingly unusual. He had been given seeds many years previously by a gardening friend and had kept growing them for their enormous peas which he said 'taste like beans'. The large black-eyed seeds even looked rather like those of broad beans. Some references to black-eyed 'marrowfat' peas occur in old texts, but it was hardly surprising that Mr Bound had not been able to find his 'bean peas' in modern catalogues. Even the pea collection in the Genetic Resources Unit at the John Innes Centre in Norwich did not have a sample which matched his, and this contains over 3000 accessions of peas from all areas of the world. There did, however, turn out to be similar large peas in the Norwegian gene bank: bönärt that apparently were once used by poor fishermen to make a special porridge.

What about yields?

Many gardeners claim that their own home-saved varieties crop as well or even better than the new ones, and this may seem surprising when modern varieties are bred for high yields. However, the growing conditions under which these varieties are developed and trialled are often much better than those in gardens. At high altitudes, when exposed to coastal winds, or on heavy wet clay, for example, old varieties may well outperform the new ones. This is particularly the case if they were once bred for a specific area, or if they have been home-saved in one place for many years. Horticulturist and author Peter Blackburne-Maze has a good example:

'Years ago, when I lived on a tough old bit of Essex clay, I remember growing a variety of Brussels sprout called Essex Wonder. Charlie Abbot who had a nursery up Manningtree way had bred it and it was the best sprout I'd ever seen there. Hard as a bullet and with a great flavour. I then moved to west Norfolk and my beloved Essex Wonder was useless – nearly all the sprouts 'blew' before they matured. The conditions, mainly the lighter soil, just didn't suit it'.

Another reason why old varieties can appear to give lower yields is that their harvest is often spread over a long period. In vegetable trials, however, it is usually the yield within a certain peak cropping time that is measured. A long harvest period is not what commercial growers want, but is usually more useful to gardeners. A few fresh pickings of runner beans in July and October are worth far more than an increased glut in August, for example, and this is the reason some seedsavers give for sticking to their old home-saved strains of this crop.

Saving money

There may have been a time when seeds were cheap and packets were fuller but generally this is no longer the case, and for allotment and community groups in particular, reducing costs can be a considerable incentive to save and swap seeds. Even for individual gardeners, the price of some seed can seem prohibitive, especially if large quantities are required. This is certainly the case for growing 'seedling crops' of lettuce, spinach, turnip or radish for example, where seeds are sown thickly and the seedlings cut for salads or stir fries when they are only a few inches high. The quantity of seed used is large compared to the small return on each, and high quality is not required. Many gardeners find it worth saving seed for such cut-and-come again crops for themselves.

Growing for show

Gardeners who regularly enter produce in the major vegetable shows often save their own seed: particularly of runner beans, onions, peas and leeks, and sometimes of other crops such as carrots. They develop their own strains which do well in the local growing conditions and also satisfy the exacting criteria of the show schedules: the largest leeks, the straightest runner beans or the best shaped onions. Sometimes these strains are closely related to modern catalogue varieties. Sometimes, however, they have been developed from old strains and home-saved for many years, using time and skills not available to commercial breeders. Along with the tricks of the trade, the seeds pass amongst other competitors as gifts, seed swaps or raffle prizes, or are advertised in the small ads in gardening magazines. Although vegetables for the show bench need to be uniform and blemish free, their flavour is not necessarily inferior – most exhibitors eat the many 'rejects' that don't make the grade, and grow varieties for taste as well as for show.

One that has already become a legend of both local and national vegetable championships is the runner bean Stenner – a long-podded, scarlet flowered variety painstakingly developed by Mr Stenner of Bridgend over many years. At Easter in 1969, a cousin called at his house and put on the table six bean seeds for him 'to try'. Their name was unknown, but when he grew them Mr Stenner saw what potential they had and kept selecting and saving seed annually. In 1974 he found a bean with 10 seeds: 'Most unusual' says Mr Stenner:

'The following year, 1975, I sowed and planted the 10 seeds to the exclusion of all other seed – just the 10 plants. I saved the seed from these 10 plants and so the Stenner strain was launched'.

He first entered Stenner runner beans in a National Vegetable Society show in 1976 where they won first prize, and the variety went on to become almost unbeatable. From that date, he says 'It is fair to say that it has dominated the runner bean classes both nationally and locally'. Mr Stenner is now over 80, and is on the point of giving up growing the bean for seed except to provide for himself and a few 'special customers', but its career is not over yet. Stewardship is passing to a fellow exhibitor and runner bean enthusiast, and Mr Stenner also donated seeds to the Heritage Seed Library.

Living heirlooms

For many varieties sent to the Seed Search project, seed had originally been given to the donors simply by erstwhile neighbours or colleagues, or by the local farmer, the town's gravedigger or the village molecatcher. Other varieties were 'heirlooms', handed down through families like a bible or piece of silver, living links to people from the past. Unlike old books or antiques, however, they cannot be left to gather dust on the shelf: the beneficiaries must sow and harvest seed as regularly as their grandfather or great aunt would have done, and there is a powerful incentive – almost a responsibility – to keep such varieties alive.

Sometimes these vegetable heirlooms go back several generations. For example, the purple-podded pea Clarke's Beltony Blue, sent to the Seed Search by Mrs Anderson of Lewes in Sussex, had been grown on her great grandfather's farm in county Tyrone back in the 1850s. Her grandfather then grew it in his own garden, followed by her father after that, and he eventually passed seed on to her. Similarly Mr Brooks from Chislehurst, himself over 70, still grows the large fleshy red tomato that his grandfather always grew. He reckons that it is at least 160 years old, taking it back to a time when tomatoes were still called 'love apples' in many catalogues and only just becoming widely appreciated.

In other cases home-saved seeds were a poignant reminder of a much valued gardening friend. For Jennifer Russell, for example, it was the broad bean grown for over 40 years by Yorkshire farm worker George Bowland that she treasured. George was an old and experienced gardener who came to help her, a total novice, to grow vegetables in her newly acquired but overgrown kitchen garden. This was a considerable honour, because she says:

> 'I've come to realise that there isn't much George doesn't know about vegetable gardening... .If I wanted to try and grow something different I would always ask his permission. He must have been highly amused at some of my dafter ideas, but I did introduce him to the delights of mangetout and he began growing them in his own garden. Once I thought I'd be clever and grow a separate variety of broad bean, but when it came to picking them, the look on George's face said it all. It was then that I first realised how excellent his variety was.'

George's health deteriorated and he moved away to a retirement flat but, says Jennifer 'I shall continue to grow them each year ...I'd like to call them Bowland's Beauty in honour of a real gem of a person who taught me so much about gardening and, more importantly, passed on his enthusiasm to me.'

A sense of history

Varieties that have some association with local history or culture, or with notable events in the past, are always popular amongst home seedsavers and are more likely to survive. Sometimes these are old catalogue varieties no longer available, such as the Prince Albert pea, introduced around the time Prince Albert married Victoria. Often, however, they have never appeared in seed catalogues. The runner bean Churchfield Black, for example, is still widely grown in gardens and allotments in the West Midlands. Samples of seed were sent to the Seed Search from as far apart as Shifnal in Shropshire to the west, and Rugby to the east. No one as yet has given the variety an exact date or origin – some say that it was named after an area of West Bromich, others that it came from a Major Churchfield who owned a large allotment site in the area – but memories of it go back well over 60 years.

According to local folklore, the dwarf French bean Brighstone had a dramatic arrival to the Isle of Wight. Fred Arnold from Sandown tells the tale:

Brighstone beans

'This variety takes its name from a village in the West Wight, which has a history of shipwrecks on the dangerous shores. The story goes that the bean seed came from a wreck before the turn of the century; local gardeners and allotment holders have grown this bean for years. I myself have been growing it for 50 years; we all save the seed each year.'

There was no hint of the history behind the tall pea Prew's Special when Mr Feltham of Dymock in Gloucestershire first sent the variety to the Seed Search. A few months later, however, he sent an intriguing postscript '...apparently the peas originated in Egypt'. So we began to investigate. Mr Feltham had been given seed by his father, who had obtained them from a friend, old Mr Prew – hence the name. However, Mr Prew had originally got the seeds from his son, who had been given them in the 1970s by a neighbour, Mr Northover, in Blandford Forum in Dorset. Mr Northover had been in his 80s then, so this long chain of seedsavers seemed likely to end there. Remarkably, however, we eventually got a letter from Mr Northover's daughter, who wrote:

'My father did, I believe, obtain these seeds from a gardener at Lord Portman's Estate at Bryanston... The son of the then Lord Portman was given the peas by Lord Carnarvon, who obtained them in 1922 when he opened the tomb of Tutankhamen.'

A few months after opening the tomb, Lord Carnarvon was dead – struck, it was said, by the mummy's curse. Not such a good variety to grow after all, you might think, but be reassured by the fact that Mr Prew who has been growing and eating them for years, is well over 80!

Reminders of home

When gardeners move – to another allotment site, another county or another country – they hang on to their own favourite vegetable varieties, which often means saving seed for themselves. Whether through nostalgia or necessity, they often keep these familiar varieties alive for many years. Thus Mr Knowlman still saves seed of the old local pea Forty First, which came with him from Devon to Gloucestershire where no-one else grew it. Nor were they likely to understand its name: 'Forty-first' he says 'is a Devonshire expression for something really good'. He can recall eating the peas at the age of four or five back in the early 1920s.

Seeds have always been in the luggage of families emigrating to other countries, and many UK crops and varieties were taken to America by early settlers because they were not available in the 'New World'; some are still kept by gene banks and seed saving networks there today. One strain of kale collected by the Seed Search was taken from this country to Canada over 150 years ago and reappeared growing in a garden in Somerset. Mrs Shuker from Bath had been given seed of the variety years ago by a Canadian girl, Nancy Stevens, whom she met when they were both working in London after the war. Mrs Shuker takes up the tale:

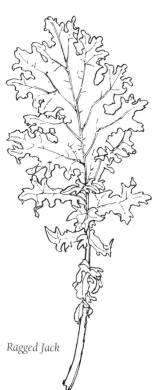

'Nancy's father emigrated as a lad of 15 somewhere around the middle of the 19th century, and his family took with them as many vegetable seeds as they could manage, among these seeds was Ragged Jack kale. When Nancy's father married, some of the family seed store was passed on to him. He had by this time settled on Saltspring island, Vancouver, and there Nancy and her brothers and sisters grew up. Each spring Ragged Jack kale was their first green vegetable to be picked after a

Ragged Jack

cold Canadian winter. It seems that the Stevens family have always taken care to keep seed from the old family stock, and on one of her visits to Canada, Nancy came into possession of a pinch which she brought back and grew on, and that is how I got mine... I have grown and propagated it right up until the present day.'

Just as families moving across the Atlantic in the 19th century took seeds with them, so the immigrant communities that settled in Britain brought in their favourite crops and varieties, and this process is still going on today. Go to any allotment site in a racially mixed community and you will see plots which bear little resemblance to the traditional rotation of brassicas, potatoes and legumes. At Uplands Allotments in Handsworth, Birmingham, 70% of the 400 plots have been taken up by Indian or West Indian gardeners, and are growing unfamiliar crops such as fenugreek, coriander, and four types of the leafy amaranth which they call calalloo. Local ethnic shops are a source of some seeds, particularly when the seeds are the part of the plant that is also eaten – coriander, grown as a spice, for example. Other seed has come from home, and is saved and passed around the site. Some of the calalloo is reputed to have originated with one of the first West Indians to come to Uplands back in the 1960s: a red-seeded type treated as a half hardy annual, and a hardier 'white calalloo'. This crop is not one that you would find on most UK allotments but it is accepted as normal here at Uplands. Item 32 on the schedule of the Autumn flower, fruit and vegetable show along with the cabbages and chrysanthemums is 'Calalloo, 10 stems judged for quality and freshness.'

A wider view

Gardeners thus have many personal reasons for keeping their old favourite vegetables in cultivation, but there are also wider issues at stake. Together the old, home-saved varieties represent a huge store of genetic material, and one that is immensely varied. Its diversity stems from the way the varieties have been adapted and selected, by all sorts of different people in different growing conditions and with different wants and needs.

Plant breeders have produced modern varieties from the old ones, but using only the characteristics they need to satisfy the immediate market. The result is varieties which are much better for commercial growers, but which have greatly depleted genetic variation. The problem comes when conditions or markets change, and other qualities are needed for the latest crops – qualities which may have only existed in strains that are now extinct. The Old Cornish cauliflower, for example, had valuable resistance to ringspot, and would have been useful in breeding programmes aimed at reducing the effect of this disease. In the 1950s, however, this strain of the crop was replaced by new 'improved' French varieties, and subsequently disappeared from cultivation.

Crimson flowered broad bean

Loss of genetic diversity can make a crop dangerously vulnerable, as history has already shown. If all the varieties widely grown are genetically identical, and a pest or disease evolves that can successfully attack them, then it will quickly devastate the whole crop. This was an underlying cause of the Irish potato famine in 1845, and occurred again later in 1970s America where an attack of leaf blight on hybrid corns caused some farmers to lose their entire harvest. While we continue to grow too few varieties all too similar to each other, such disasters could happen again in the future.

It is the wild relatives of crops in tropical and subtropical regions that show most genetic diversity, together with the relatively undeveloped landraces cultivated by subsistence farmers, and it is essential to keep these for the future. Although national gene banks can be valuable, far more so are community seed banks and programmes to help local farmers grow and maintain their traditional crops. This is a far more sustainable approach to tackling poverty than the adoption of modern farming techniques and new hybrid crops.

Nevertheless, even our old garden varieties can be genetically unique and have an important role to play. Some scientific proof of this came recently when Dr D. A. Bond of Cambridge carried out a series of investigations with the Crimson Flowered broad bean – a favourite from the Heritage Seed Library collection. A few seeds were given to HDRA back in the 1970s by an elderly lady, Miss Cutbush of Kent, whose father had grown them on their family farm since the 1920s (p66). References to crimson-flowered beans appear in early literature but they do not feature in popular Victorian or 20th century catalogues, and all broad beans sold to gardeners now have predominantly white flowers. Dr Bond established that the crimson colour was an independent gene or 'allele' and that it had never before been found or named in the scientific literature.

The crimson flower 'gene' makes itself obvious, producing a stunningly beautiful plant, but who knows what equally important but less visual characteristics remain undiscovered in other old varieties – in the Heritage Seed Library or in your back garden? They may be scorned by plant breeders today, but they might be needed tomorrow.

Doing it yourself

For some gardeners, therefore, it is the taste or performance of the old strains that makes seed saving worthwhile, or the strong associations that they have with people or places from the past. For others it is simply that saving seeds saves money, or that by growing and maintaining a range of old varieties they are helping to bring about a small increase in biodiversity. For many, however, it is the sheer satisfaction that seed saving gives – linking season to season and year to year, as generations of gardeners have done in the past. Mrs Wilson from Suffolk, who saves seed of the old climbing French bean Caseknife for the Heritage Seed Library, certainly has this feeling:

'Being a Seed Guardian is such a pleasure in this day of speed, computerisation, and stress. Watching a seed germinate, grow, feed you and then reproduce enough of itself to carry on year after year is a miracle we should all take more seriously. If man lived by seasons more as he once did we could all possibly survive as Caseknife has, to the age of 180!'

Heritage Seed Search volunteer Jan Peters helping to bag carrot flowers to isolate them from pollinating insects.

Seed saving techniques

For some crops, seed saving is very simple. Peas are a good example: the part of the plant that you eat is also the seed, so by the time you have grown peas for the table you are almost there. It is also easy to keep pea varieties pure, and to get seed ripe enough to harvest even in short growing seasons.

For other crops, seed saving may take more forethought and sometimes needs special techniques. Plants may have to be overwintered before they set seed, or they may have to be protected to get a long enough growing season. Individual varieties may also have to be isolated in some way to keep the seed true to type. Once you are familiar with the needs of the various crops, however, seed saving is generally not difficult and like other aspects of gardening it can be addictive!

Gardeners often hesitate to save seeds because they think that it might be inferior to seed that comes professionally grown and packeted. However, this is not usually the case – and in fact it can often be the opposite. Sometimes gardeners growing small quantities of seed have more control over harvest conditions than commercial seed growers – they can protect plants from the rain or frost, for example, and harvest individual seedheads at their peak. This can considerably affect the seed quality. Similarly, the hands-on ways that gardeners clean small quantities of seed can sometimes be less damaging than the mechanical methods used by the companies.

What you need to know before attempting to save the seed of any crop is: how much space it will take up, how long it will take to produce seed, and what if anything you need to do to keep the variety pure.

The plant's biological clock

Some vegetables are annuals: if you sow them in spring, they will grow on to produce flowers and seeds and then die in that same year. Lettuce, peas, and French and broad beans are a few of the many vegetables that come into this category. Seed saving from these crops fits in well with the normal pattern of growing crops to eat, although you must allow for the plants to be in the ground for longer – until the seed is ready for harvesting. Where the growing season is short, some of these crops may need to be started off in a greenhouse or polytunnel in order to give them time to produce dry ripe seed; occasionally it may even be best to grow them to maturity inside.

The majority of other crops are biennials: they take two growing seasons to produce seed, and then they die. Main crop onions, root crops such as carrots and parsnips, and brassicas such as Brussels sprouts and kale are all biennials. Normally in the first growing season they form the part of the vegetable that we eat, and only if they are left to experience a period of winter cold will they then go on to flower and produce seed. Thus biennial crops grown for seed use up space for much longer, but there are compensations: some of the flowers – the white umbels of the carrot and the architectural spheres of the onion, for example, can look surprisingly attractive and are loved by bees and other beneficial insects.

Perennial vegetables are those which go on growing year after year, and they are often multiplied in other ways as well as – or instead of – from seed. They include those that are grown in permanent beds such as asparagus and globe artichokes, and others that are dug up each year and propagated from tubers or offsets such as potatoes or shallots. Some frost-tender plants that are actually perennials in their country of origin, such as runner beans and tomatoes, are treated as annuals in our climate.

Getting a good start

Plants for seed saving are generally raised in the same way as those for edible crops. However, sometimes it may be beneficial to start seed off inside – even seed of crops that you would normally sow directly outside in the garden. It helps to improve the germination rate, which is valuable if you have been given very small numbers of seeds, for example, or if you suspect the seed is old and lacking in vigour. It also helps you to get an early start, and hence an early seed harvest, for crops such as lettuce and French beans which might otherwise be ruined by autumn weather.

One important rule is never to sow all the seed that you have of one variety. Disasters can easily happen: the plants might be caught by an unexpected frost or demolished by slugs, and with a home-saved variety you can't usually just go out and buy more. Even after the seed has been collected, things can go wrong. Such a near catastrophe happened to the two sisters saving Cyril's Choice tomato – a variety which they were keeping in cultivation in memory of their brother Cyril who had grown it for many years before he died. One year, they did not dry the seed properly and thought they had lost the variety for good, but on searching they found two old seeds caught in the bottom ridges of the tin in which they kept their seed packets. Thus Cyril's Choice was saved (and is now in the Heritage Seed Library) – but more by luck than good practice. Better to have kept back a small batch of the previous year's seed, carefully labelled and stored.

Sowing in pots and modules

All seeds need warmth, moisture and air to germinate: cold and waterlogging are the main enemies. If you have a greenhouse, you can start seeds off in pots, trays or modules filled with a good quality multipurpose compost. Modules are trays divided into cells in which seeds can be sown and individual plants raised. These minimise the shock of transplanting and enable you to sow even crops like beetroot, carrots and parsnips inside. A propagator or heated bench which provides heat directly to the underside of the pot or tray is ideal, particularly for seeds that need higher temperatures to germinate such as French beans.

Beetroot sown in modules

Pre-germination

Another way to start off large seeds such as peas, beans and squashes is to 'pre-germinate' them. Spread the seeds out thinly on moist paper towelling in a flat plastic container and put it in a propagator or other warm place. An airing cupboard can be suitable, but make sure it is not too hot: 20°C is about right for most seeds. Check the container daily and make sure the seeds are still moist. Once the tiny shoots emerge, they can be sown either in pots or trays in the greenhouse, or directly outside. Handle them very carefully to avoid damaging the shoots.

Pre-germination can also be used for small seeds such as lettuce or parsnip, but once they have germinated they are difficult to sow without damage. For small numbers of seed use tweezers or the tip of a plant label. Larger numbers can be 'fluid sown' by stirring them into a gel made from ground up water-retaining granules mixed with water. This protects the small shoots whilst you spread the gel along a seed drill outside.

Labelling

Labelling is particularly important if you are saving your own seed and passing it on to others, partly to make sure that it is correctly named, and partly in case there are any problems with seed purity. Mark each batch of seed being pre-germinated or sown inside with the name and date and keep it labelled when you plant it outside in the garden.

Planting

Sometimes plants need to be spaced further apart for a seed crop than you would normally expect. This may be simply to allow room for the flower spikes, or to prevent plants from getting muddled with neighbouring ones so that 'roguing' (removal of off-types) is easier. Wider spacings can help prevent fungal diseases, and help air to circulate to dry the seeds.

It is surprising how large ordinary vegetable plants can get when you leave them to run to seed: the small innocuous radishes which transform themselves, like Frankenstein's monster, to metre-tall plants with many brittle, entangled branches. Often they need staking. Some guidance on planting distances is given in the crop-by-crop seed saving sections, although these will vary with variety and growing conditions so it pays to experiment. With some crops, you also have to balance the advantages of wider spacings with a noticeable drop in seed yield for a given area.

Overwintering biennial crops

As already explained, biennial plants need a period of winter cold to stimulate them to go up to seed the following summer. For home seed saving in the garden, they are normally grown during the first year in the same way as an edible crop. Hardy crops such as parsnips and kale can then be left in the ground overwinter. Less hardy root crops such as beetroot and carrots can be lifted if necessary and stored in moist leafmould or sand in a cool frost-free place and replanted the following spring. This is sometimes called the 'root-to-seed' method of seed production.

However, plants do not necessarily have to be fully mature before a period of cold will make them flower. With some crops it is possible to sow them in late summer and overwinter immature plants – with protection if necessary – and still collect seed the following year. This is sometimes called the 'seed-to-seed' method. Its advantage is that it occupies space for less time, and you do not have to store and re-establish roots, which occasionally can be a problem. The disadvantage is that you cannot observe the plants in their normal growing conditions, and there are not the same opportunities for roguing and selection (see p42).

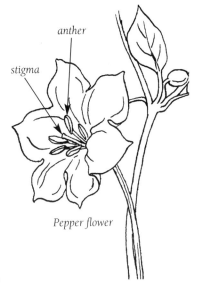

Pepper flower

Pollination

To produce viable seed, flowers must be pollinated: the stigma of the flower (the receptive female part) must receive pollen from the anthers (the productive male part) either of the same or of a different flower. The pollen then travels from the stigma to the ovary of the flower where fertilisation of the 'ovules' or female egg cells occurs. Both the male pollen and female ovules carry genetic information which contributes to the final make-up of the seed. When you are seed saving, you need to know a little about how pollination occurs for different crops.

A flower is 'self-pollinated' if pollen is transferred from anthers to stigma within the same flower: that is, the one flower provides both parents for the seed. It is cross-pollinated if pollen is brought from another flower, usually by wind or by insects. If this pollen comes from another flower on the same plant or on another plant of the same variety, then the resultant seed will give plants that are true to type. If, however, the pollen comes from a flower of a different variety then the resultant seed will carry traits from both varieties and the plants which you

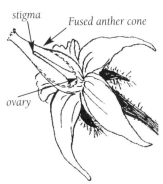

In a tomato flower the anthers are fused together to form a cone around the stigma

grow from it the following year can look different from both parents. Squashes can show this with dramatic effect: seeds from a small round yellow fruit producing something long and green, or large and orange, because of cross-pollination in the previous generation.

Crops which nearly always self-pollinate are called 'inbreeders', and these are the easiest to keep pure. In peas, for example, self-pollination usually occurs before the flowers are even open, making any cross-pollination unlikely. At the other extreme there are brassicas, where for a flower to set seed it must have pollen brought by insects not just from a different flower but from a flower on a different plant. There is a physiological mechanism which prevents pollen fertilising flowers on the same plant (this is called 'self-incompatibility'). So if you leave just one odd cabbage to flower on your vegetable plot, you will get little if any seed. Crops like this which naturally cross-pollinate most of the time are called 'outbreeders'.

In between these extremes are crops which do a bit of both self- and cross-pollination. A pepper flower, for example, readily self-pollinates but cross-pollination by insects can occur as well. An onion flower rarely self-pollinates, but only because its pollen is released before the stigma is ready to receive it – there is no self-incompatibility and the pollen can, and often does, come from another flower on the same plant. Onion flowers are described by plant breeders as 'protandrous'. In all these examples, the plants have both male and female parts within the same flower. This is most commonly the case with vegetables, but not always. Sometimes crops have separate male and female flowers. In squashes and sweetcorn, for example, male and female flowers are separate but both types of flower occur on every plant. In spinach and asparagus, there are separate male and female plants each producing only one type of flower.

Keeping varieties pure

Clearly, if you want pure seed of a particular variety you have to prevent foreign pollen from fertilising the flowers. Only plants of the same species are a threat. Thus the runner beans (*Phaseolus coccineus*) that you are growing will not cross naturally with any French beans (*Phaseolus vulgaris*) but are likely to cross with other runner bean varieties on your plot or on any nearby ones. Similarly celery (*Apium graveolens*) will not cross with lovage (*Levisticum officinale*), however similar the plants look, but it will cross with celeriac (also *Apium graveolens*). For some vegetables, pollen from weeds or agricultural crops can also be a problem. Wild carrot (*Daucus carota*) will cross with cultivated carrots (also *Daucus carota*), for example, and sugar beet (*Beta vulgaris*) with garden beetroot. From this standpoint, gardeners in the city who are saving seeds can sometimes be better off than those in country areas.

There are two common ways of isolating a seed crop to prevent contamination: either isolating by distance (making sure that there are no other varieties of the same crop nearby) or by using a physical barrier.

Isolation distances

The 'isolation distance' – how near you can grow two varieties together without cross-pollination – varies from crop to crop. Those which usually self-pollinate before insects get a look in, such as peas and French beans, can be grown much closer together than the promiscuous outbreeders such as kales and cabbages. However, the isolation distance will also depend on the site, how the pollen is carried, and even on the year.

The majority of crops which we grow in our gardens are insect pollinated, and for these the isolation distance will depend mostly on:

- How many and what types of insect pollinators there are.
- What physical barriers there are between the crop you are saving and any other varieties of the same crop (or other plants of the same species).
- How many plants you are growing.
- What other sources of nectar and pollen there are to waylay the insects in between.

This means that when crops are grown for seed commercially in large fields with only sparse hedges, or are grown on open allotment sites, they are likely to need a larger isolation distance than they would in a garden, where there are buildings, trees, thick hedges, tall plants and many other flowers to interrupt the insects' flight path. Such barriers are less effective for blocking the pollen of wind pollinated plants such as beetroot and sweetcorn, however, and it is much harder to reduce the isolation distances for these crops.

You can sometimes reduce isolation distances by growing a large number of plants – preferably set out in a block rather than a row. This reduces the probability of any individual flower outcrossing, and seed collected just from the centre of the block is even more likely to be pure, as insects will not carry foreign pollen far into the crop. However, you can only afford to grow enough plants to discard seed from the outer ones if you have plenty of space and enough seed to start with. Flowers of other species – vegetable or ornamental – planted between the two blocks may also attract the insects and prevent outcrossing, but it is difficult to be sure how effective this will be. Some seed savers report watching bees go from a kale crop grown for seed to flowering sage plants nearby, for example, rather than travel to the flowers of the next kale variety. However, there is also evidence to suggest the opposite – that bees get a 'taste' for particular flowers and collect only from one type until these are used up.

Determining an effective isolation distance for any crop is therefore not straightforward, and usually depends on the amount of crossing that can be tolerated. The recent controversy over trials of genetically modified crops has highlighted just how far pollen can actually travel; oilseed rape pollen has been recorded 4km from the crop, for example. The advised isolation distances for commercial seed crops are not as great as this, but are still a long way in gardening terms: usually of the order of 300-1000m for outbreeding crops, depending on the crop and the standard of seed required.

Recommendations suggested for commercial seed growers are given in the Crop-by-Crop Seed Saving chapters, and if you are growing seed for passing on to other gardeners you really should be guided by these. They may be large, but they are not necessarily restrictive. Biennial vegetables such as carrots, onions and brassicas grown for eating are usually harvested long before they flower. As long as you grow only one variety for seed in any one year, you can grow other varieties for the kitchen, and you do not normally have to worry about contamination from your neighbours' crops.

It is broad and runner beans which flower before giving an edible crop which are the most problem. For pure seed you really do need a large distance between your seed crop and other varieties that you or your neighbours are growing. Frank Clark, who has been saving a family heirloom broad bean for 50 years (p7) is lucky – he lives on an isolated smallholding in the hills. Most people have many neighbours. One way to get around this might be to persuade your neighbours to grow the same variety by giving them seeds or plants. This is how the white-flowered runner bean Fry was kept true to type when it was grown out for the Seed Search: the neighbours were only too pleased to help, even more so after the variety won prizes at the village show!

If you are just growing seed for your own use, however, and have stock seed in reserve, you can afford to experiment with much shorter isolation distances. Remember that factors such as numbers of plants, intervening buildings and hedges, and the direction of the prevailing wind will have an effect. As long as you are familiar with the variety, you should easily be able to recognise any markedly different 'rogue' plants that appear in the next generation as a result of crossing. At first, try using varieties where such rogues are obvious – a white flowered runner bean where all the neighbouring varieties have red flowers, for example, or the Crimson-flowered broad bean (see p66). This will help make you confident of the level of seed purity you can expect from plants on your own plot.

Physical barriers

The alternative to isolating a seed crop by distance is to use a physical barrier that will prevent insect pollinators reaching the flowers. A decade ago old net curtains were one of the few suitable materials available for DIY barriers, but now there are a whole range of horticultural fleeces and types of fine mesh netting on the market. These are designed to protect crops from insect pests and are hence ideal for isolation purposes. Although they keep out insects, they will let through light, air and moisture. Polythene is not suitable for making impenetrable barriers, as the heat and moisture created is likely to cause flowers on the crop inside to rot. Fine mesh netting is usually preferable to horticultural fleece for long periods of use in summer as it allows more air circulation to the crop.

Bagged pepper flower

Bagging

If you only want small quantities of seed, simply putting bags over individual flowers or flower trusses may be all that is needed. You can make the bags from fleece or mesh, or from the perforated cellophane used to wrap bread in supermarkets. Secure the neck of the bag round the stalk with string or a twist of soft wire – you may need to wrap cotton wool around the stalk underneath to fill gaps that small insects might use to crawl through. Once flowering inside the bags has finished, mark the trusses that have been isolated and remove the bags. Tomatoes and peppers are examples of crops where this method works well.

Caging

Alternatively you can put barriers round whole plants or groups of plants. These can be anything from makeshift structures of canes and fleece to custom-built cages of wood or piping covered with mesh. You could also use the proprietary metal 'vegetable cages' usually sold to keep off birds, substituting a fine insect-excluding material for

Plants isolated from pollinating insects

the ordinary netting. Whatever the level of sophistication of your insect-proof cage, cover the plants before they start to flower. Make sure there are no gaps in the cover, and dig loose fleece or netting into the ground at the base or weight it down firmly. Also ensure that the plants have plenty of space so that the flowers do not touch the cover at the top or sides; if they do, insects may try and work the flowers through the material and contamination could occur. Once flowering has finished, mark the plants that have been isolated then remove the cage, or make sure it is well ventilated to help ripen and dry the seed. On a larger scale, the Heritage Seed Library uses mesh-covered polytunnels, and greenhouses where the door and vents have been covered with mesh.

Physical isolation works well for plants whose flowers will self pollinate in the absence of insects, but some crops need these insects to move pollen from flower to flower before they will set seed. Sometimes you can do the insects' work yourself by hand: it is fairly simple to successfully hand pollinate individual squash flowers for example – and quite fun (see p41). Isolated onion and carrot flowerheads can be pollinated by brushing them with a fine paintbrush or with the palm of your hand to transfer pollen, and runner beans can also be hand pollinated. However, what is easy for insects is not always easy for us! The timing must be right for example, and hand-pollination can also be a drawn out job as the flowers open over a long period. It is important to move pollen from plant to plant as well as from flower to flower on the same plant, and each time you remove the bags or cages, you must prevent nearby insects getting there first. Hardly surprisingly, hand pollination rarely gives such a good set as insect pollination.

Using blowflies

An option used by commercial seed producers is to introduce insects into the isolation cages: hives of bees are used for runner beans, for example, and flies for brassicas, onions and carrots. Whereas bees are not something gardeners can usually consider, it is possible to try blowflies. You can introduce these as maggots or their pupae ('castors'), which you can buy at fishing shops.

You will probably find that blowfly maggots are sold by the pint (loose, so take a container). Half a pint is normally the minimum you can buy, and this will be plenty for the number of plants you are likely to be growing in a garden or on an allotment. Although you may get quizzical looks, it is wise to admit to the shopkeeper what you are using the maggots for, as some that are sold may not go on to complete their lifecycle. Normally, however, they change from maggots to pupae within a few days, and from pupae to flies in one to two weeks (about one week at 18°C, longer at lower temperatures). The best time to get the maggots is therefore a week or so before flowering starts. Spread them out in a container which will keep rain out, but has holes to let the flies escape. Put this somewhere warm until the maggots have turned into pupae and then put it in the cage. The flies have a relatively short lifetime, and where flowering continues over a long period, you may have to reintroduce more after a few weeks to keep up the numbers.

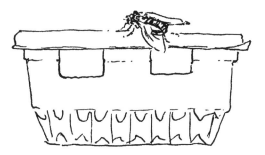

Simple boxes for introducing blowfly maggots into isolation cages can be made from old margarine containers.

Alternate day caging

Even using introduced insects, plants isolated inside a physical barrier often set less seed than those pollinated naturally outside. Where the foreign pollen is likely to come from your neighbour's vegetable plot or from agricultural crops, however, there is little alternative. If there are no external sources of pollen but you want to grow two varieties for seed yourself, you can get round the pollination problem by caging them on alternate days – swapping the cages around at night while there are no insects around. While the first variety is caged, insects can pollinate the second and vice versa.

Isolation and hand-pollination of cucurbit flowers

Cucumber, marrow and squash plants usually have separate male and female flowers, easily distinguished because each female flower has a tiny immature fruit behind it, whereas male flowers sit on straight stalks. The first that appear are usually male, but female flowers should soon start to appear. Watch them vigilantly.

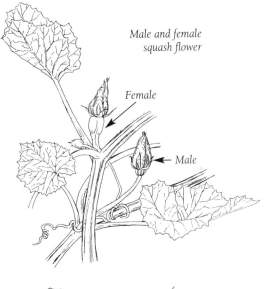

*Male and female
squash flower*

Female

Male

- Select both male and female flowers that are just about to open – they will be mostly green but showing yellow around the tip. The flowers can be on the same plant or, preferably, on different plants of the same variety. The more plants you grow, the more chance you have of finding male and female flowers ready to open at the same time.
- Enclose each of these flowers in a bag of perforated cellophane (you can re-use the wrapping supermarkets often use for bread), allowing the flowers room to open. Use string or a twist of soft wire to secure it around the stem.
- The next day, remove the covering from a male flower that has opened. Pick the flower and gently tear off the petals to expose the pollen-bearing stamen. Then take the bag off an opened female flower. Brush the male stamen onto the central stigma of the female flower – the pollen should stick to it – then rebag the flower quickly. Bees find cucurbit flowers so attractive that they are likely to sneak in right under your nose!
- Repeat for other flowers – you can use the same male flower to pollinate more than one female at the same time if necessary.

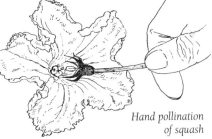

*Hand pollination
of squash*

You can finally take away the bags when the pollinated flowers drop off and the fruit start to swell. Leave a piece of string or tape round the stems of these fruit so that later you can identify them from others that have not been isolated. With vigorous trailing varieties, it can also help to put a cane by the hand-pollinated fruits so that you can find them amongst the mass of foliage.

Plant numbers, roguing and selection

Plants of any open-pollinated (as opposed to hybrid) variety will vary slightly from each other: in appearance, harvest time, hardiness and other characteristics. For example, the first plants of an open-pollinated broccoli to produce spears ready for eating may do this several weeks before the last plant is ready to harvest. In varieties from seed catalogues these variations will be small, because legally they have to conform to a certain standard of uniformity (see p18). However, home-saved varieties may show greater variability. A 'landrace' – an early cultivated form of a crop, bred and maintained by farmers or rural communities – is likely to show the most variation even in obvious characteristics, such as the colour pattern on French bean seeds.

This variation is generally beneficial, as it gives varieties the potential to adapt to a range of conditions, and for this reason it is important to try and maintain it in future generations. On the other hand, you do not want plants that lack the essential characteristics of the variety, or that are inferior in some way, to contribute to the next generation.

Selecting plants for seed saving is a balance between keeping the genetic diversity, and eliminating undesirable characteristics ('roguing' the crop) to keep the variety true-to-type, and this is something that becomes easier with experience. There are a few basic rules to start with:

- The crop must be grown well – at the correct time and spacing for the variety and in good growing conditions – otherwise it is impossible to rogue or select effectively.
- Save seed from as many plants of the variety as you can. This is particularly important for outbreeding crops such as brassicas where it helps shuffle the genes and prevent 'inbreeding depression': if too few plants are grown, the variety loses its variation and often becomes weak and susceptible to disease. It is less important for naturally inbreeding crops such as peas, which have a different genetic structure and less variability between plants. If you found two pea seeds of an old variety in the back of a drawer, for example, provided they germinated and grew, you could probably re-establish the variety. You could not do this if you found only two kale or cabbage seeds, however. Suggested minimum numbers of plants are given in the crop-by-crop seed saving chapters.
- Never save seed from plants that are weak or show signs of disease. Some diseases can be carried over in the seed. Check plants regularly and remove suspect plants as soon as possible.
- Do not save seed from plants that have undesirable traits. For example, reject lettuce plants that are the first to produce flower spikes – seeds from these plants are likely to give lettuces that also bolt early, shortening the harvest period. With annual outbreeding crops, remove the undesirable plants as soon as possible,

before any cross-pollination occurs. With inbreeding or biennial crops, you can afford to wait and eat the rejects!

- Do not save seed from odd plants that are obviously very different from the rest, and that do not fit in with the descriptions of the variety that you are trying to save. Otherwise in future generations the variety will start to lose its essential characteristics. It is particularly important to be aware of this for outbreeding crops. If you are saving the Crimson-flowered broad bean, for example, where the main identifiable characteristic of the variety is its beautiful red flowers then any plants with off-colour flowers are obviously not acceptable, and because broad beans cross-pollinate, they should be removed as soon as possible. Try to observe the plants in all stages of growth, and look at all parts of them, not just the visually obvious ones or the bits that you eat. For example, with tomatoes look at the shape of the leaves as well as the fruit.

After you have eliminated all the inferior plants in this way, you may still have to make a choice of plants to save for seed. To maintain the innate variability of the variety, it is important to look at all the characteristics of the plants, not just the obvious ones which affect the edible parts. It is all to easy to accidentally select for large tomatoes or early maturing beans, for example, when in fact this is not a characteristic you particularly require. If you pregerminate lots of seed and only plant out the first ones to germinate, you may also be making an unwarranted selection.

If you do select for one particular characteristic, such as size or earliness in a variety, you will be deliberately creating your own strain over the years. It is a valid alternative approach to seed saving, but if you are giving seed to anyone else, you should make it clear what you have done. This is what John Purves did when he wanted a purple carrot (p72), and what Mr Stenner did when he bred his Stenner Strain runner bean (p154).

Of course, generally some selection beyond your control is going on all the time, because of the particular growing conditions in your garden or on your allotment. Plants that do well under these conditions will contribute proportionately more seed to your harvest each time, and so the variety will gradually adapt. Hence the benefit of having local varieties supplied locally as in times past. If you were trying to husband the variety to maintain all its diversity, as a gene bank should do, you would have to try and overcome this local adaptation by saving equal amounts of seed from every disease-free plant, regardless of how it performed.

Whatever your selection, mark the plants that you are using for seed saving clearly, especially if other people are gardening on or harvesting from the plot. 'This year the plants escaped the snails' said one letter to the Heritage Seed Library 'Unfortunately they didn't escape being pulled up by mum, so I am left to dream about the wonders of this lettuce.' Most seedsavers have their own method of indicating to long-suffering family members that those beans are not to be eaten and those bolting lettuces are not to be put on the compost heap. One even goes as far as wrapping Christmas tinsel around her plants! White markers on canes or coloured insulating tape or string are among the most practical suggestions.

The seed harvest

Even for annual vegetables, it can be weeks after the edible stage before the crop produces ripe seed, and it is important to be patient and wait for the seeds to mature on the plant. This applies both to seeds contained in fruit pulp such as those of tomatoes and courgettes, and those harvested dry from pods or capsules such as beans, brassicas and lettuce.

The time you have to wait depends on the crop. Tomato and melon seeds, for example, are ready when the fruit are at the same stage as we like to eat them. Courgettes, however, are very immature when we pick them to eat; for seed saving they need several more weeks on the plant to grow to full size and then more time after that to mature.

The maturity of seeds from pods or capsules is generally indicated by a change in colour and texture; for example, pea seeds are mature when the pods start to turn pale brown and parchment-like. Ideally they should be left on the plant in the garden until they are dry, to the stage when seedheads will rustle and pods crack and rattle. Some crops, such as lettuce and carrots, have seeds which mature over a long period and unless you collect them regularly, ripe seeds will 'shatter' – that is, they will be spontaneously released from the seedheads and will be lost. To avoid this, you can go round the plants periodically, rubbing off ripe seed into a paper bag.

If the weather is continually wet or if frost threatens, individual mature pods or whole plants can be pulled up and brought in to a warm dry airy place. Lay them in trays or hang them inside paper sacks to catch any seed that is released. Bringing in whole plants or seed stalks enables the seeds that are not quite ready to continue to draw from the plant for a short time, and provided they have already reached a certain stage, they will continue to ripen and dry.

It is not always easy to find an appropriate area for drying seeds. You could hang the plants in a well-ventilated shed or empty greenhouse, for example, but make sure that it does not get too hot (the temperature should never get higher than 35°C), and beware of mice eating the seeds. Mature seed pods or seedheads could be set out in a thin layer on trays or sheets in a spare room if you have space. Mrs Whiteley from Lancashire who sent the old tall pea Duke of Albany to the Seed Search project gets round the problem by threading one end of the mature pods on strong cotton and hanging them up across the kitchen to dry.

Seed cleaning

Seed needs to be free from bits of pod and other debris before it is finally dried and stored. If you are saving seed just for your own use, it is perhaps not so important to clean it quite so thoroughly as commercial seed, but clean seed is likely to keep longer and be less likely to carry over disease. Which method of cleaning you use will depend very much on the crop, and also on the quantity of seed that you have to deal with.

Seed harvested wet from fruit will need washing in order to get rid of any pulp or gel clinging to it, and sometimes this is so persistent that special treatment is needed to remove it – as is the case with tomato seed, for example (see p171). Only then can the seed be dried.

Most seed, however, is harvested dry from pods, capsules or seedheads. 'Threshing' is the traditional way of breaking such seeds away from their coverings, and commercially this is carried out by machine. Some suggested DIY alternatives to threshing have included beating a pillowcase of dry pods with a stick, or using a rolling pin, or jogging up and down on it. You need to be careful, however, because too much pressure can damage the seeds.

In practice, with the quantities of seed you are likely to save from the garden it is usually easier to pod and separate large seeds by hand. This has the added advantage of good quality control: you can discard any seed that is malformed, damaged or off-colour at the same time. Until machines were invented that could pick out such seeds, this was the way it was done commercially. An account of pea cleaning the 1920s describes how ladies sat on wooden benches in an unheated warehouse '...wrapped in a cocoon of assorted clothing (supplemented by sacks on the worst days), their eyes fixed on the dry peas on the table immediately in front of them, their mitten-clad chilblained hands darting forward to remove any discoloured or damaged peas as they were noticed'. For small amounts of home-grown peas and beans, however, picking over the seeds can be a pleasing task.

Small quantities of tinier seeds such as brassicas and lettuce can also be broken out of their coverings by hand – by rubbing them between your finger tips in a bowl or paper bag, but the seed then needs to be separated from the 'chaff' – the bits of seed pod and other debris. This can be done by sieving or by 'winnowing' (using a gentle current of air to blow it away), or by a combination of the two.

A sieve with a mesh size just big enough to let through the seed will allow you to catch and dispose of large debris. This leaves you with the seeds and the chaff smaller than the seeds, which can be separated with a small gauge sieve. Sometimes it can take

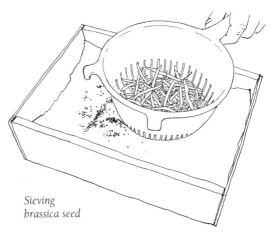

*Sieving
brassica seed*

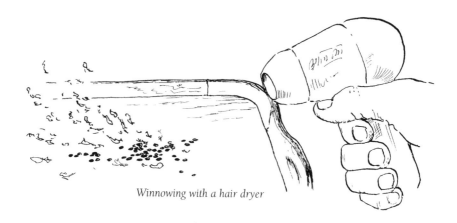

Winnowing with a hair dryer

several operations with different sieves to get the seed really clean. Specialised equipment is difficult to find and expensive to buy, so keep a look out for colanders and sieves of different sizes in kitchen shops. Alternatively, you might be able to improvise. Mrs Fardell from Cornwall, one of the volunteers helping with the Seed Search project, cleaned her whole harvest of cabbage seed with a large sieve (about 60cm x 35cm) made from cardboard with holes punched in it.

For seeds which are noticeably heavier than the chaff, winnowing can work well. Many seedsavers have their own variations of this technique. Some spread the seed/chaff mixture out and blow on it or use a fan or hair dryer. The strength of the air current will be trial and error at first, so make sure you can catch escaping seeds, which have an astonishing ability to get away: you can spread the mixture on a tray with a solid lip, for example, or on a board placed over a large sheet of paper. Eddie Lancaster from Northamptonshire, an experienced seedsaver for the Heritage Seed Library, recommends working with small amounts at a time: 'not much more than a teaspoonful' for small seeds such as lettuce. An alternative method is to shake the seed gently on a large sheet of paper until the lighter chaff comes to the surface and can be funnelled away, or to pour the seed from one deep container to another in a gentle draught of air.

Whichever method you use, seed cleaning can create a lot of dust and other particles, so always do it in a well ventilated place and *WEAR A DUST MASK.* Various grades of mask can be bought from agricultural suppliers.

Seed drying and storage

Newly harvested and cleaned seed may need further drying before you store it: seed harvested wet from fruit certainly will, and large seeds such as peas and beans are likely to still have a high moisture content. Never try to dry seeds too quickly at too high a temperature, but spread them out in a warm airy place out of strong sunlight. An airing cupboard, warm windowsill, or empty well-ventilated greenhouse are all possible places, but check the temperature – it should never get higher than 35°C or the seeds can be damaged. Put wet seeds such as those from tomatoes or squashes on a shiny surface – a plate or plastic tray, for example – so they do not irretrievably stick to it as they dry.

You can tell roughly how dry a seed is by how brittle it has become: a dry seed will snap rather than bend, or shatter rather than squash when hit with a hammer. You can also make a quick test of peas and beans by pressing on them with your thumbnail or biting on them: you should not be able to make an impression on the seed coat. When the seeds are dry, put them in paper envelopes (the sturdy 'wage packets' sold in stationers are good for small seeds). Label each packet clearly with the variety and year of harvest.

How long do seeds keep?

Lawrence Hills once wrote a memorable rhyme to help gardeners sort out their seed packets at the end of the year. It was in the lilting style of the 16th century countryman and farmer Thomas Tusser (see p12):

> '...Throw out ye Parsnip, 'tis no good next year,
> And Scorzonera if there's any there,
> For these have a life that is gone with ye wynde
> Unlike all ye seeds of ye cabbagy kind.
>
> Broccoli, Cauliflower, Sprouts, Cabbage and Kale,
> Live long like the farmer who knoweth good ale:
> Three years for certain, maybe five or four,
> To sow in their season they stay in ye drawer.'

...and so on. It illustrates well how the natural lifetime of seeds varies from crop to crop. Parsnip seeds are indeed notoriously short lived, as are those of onions. In contrast, the lifetimes of brassica and tomato seeds tend to be much longer. However, there are no hard and fast figures, because actual seed lifetimes can be affected by a number of factors including: the growing conditions of the seed crop; the harvest conditions; mechanical damage to the seed during cleaning and drying; and the storage conditions. Provided you have grown your crop on a reasonably fertile vegetable plot, and the seed has been harvested, dried and cleaned properly as described in the previous pages, the main limiting factor on its lifetime is likely to be the storage conditions.

Storing seeds

Seeds keep best in a dry, cool dark place where both the temperature and moisture levels are as constant as possible – in other words, the exact opposite conditions to those needed for germination. In practice, the damp is more of an enemy than temperature: seed kept dry at room temperature will keep viable for longer than damp seed at a low temperature.

If seeds are kept as the rhyme suggests 'in ye drawer' – in paper packets in a reasonably cool dry place such as a pantry or spare room – their lifetime will probably be on a very rough average around three years. Many tantalising packages have been sent to the Heritage Seed Library containing seed still in pre-war seed packets – found in sheds or attics, or down the backs of chairs – or even from older caches revealed behind bricks or plaster during building renovation. Unfortunately the relatively damp conditions that these seeds have experienced mean that they will almost never germinate.

However, longer lifetimes can be achieved if seeds are thoroughly dried and then prevented from taking up moisture from the atmosphere by putting them in an airtight container. One easy way of doing this at home is to use the desiccant silica gel which can be obtained from some chemists or from some laboratory or educational suppliers. The silica gel crystals are usually dyed with cobalt chloride, which makes them turn from blue when dry to pink when wet, so it is easy to see what is happening. Wide-necked Kilner jars which come with their own rubber seals are one of the best airtight storage containers, but you could use other glass jars with metal lids and make your own rubber seals. Smearing vaseline around the seals makes them more airtight.

Place your seeds in paper envelopes inside the jar together with some silica gel crystals tied in bag made of muslin or horticultural fleece. This enables you to see the colour of the crystals. If you have enough silica gel, use about the same weight of crystals as you have seed packets and envelopes – you can use less, but you will have to replace the silica gel more frequently. Once the crystals have turned pink, remove them and dry them by placing them in a very low oven 95°C for a few hours until they turn back to blue. They can then be reused. You can tell when your seeds are dry enough, because the silica gel in the jar with them will stop turning pink, and you can remove most of it and just leave a small bag (containing two or three teaspoonfuls) to indicate that the low moisture level is being maintained.

Dry seeds kept in such airtight containers and put in the fridge at about 4°C will probably have a lifetime of about seven years, maybe even longer. This extended storage life can be particularly useful for back-up batches of home-saved seed, and also for those of crops that are difficult to save as it means that you do not have to collect seed too often. When you want to remove a few seeds from a batch in cold storage, allow the jar and its contents to come to room temperature before opening it, otherwise water vapour condensing on the cold surfaces of the jar and packets will ruin you efforts to keep the seeds dry. Before sowing the seeds, you should allow them to rest for a few days at room temperature and normal humidity, as there is evidence that letting them slowly absorb water during this period is less damaging than putting them directly into moist soil. Don't try putting seeds in the freezer as this can damage them unless they are really dry.

However, national gene banks have the facilities to keep seeds longer in even more extreme conditions. At the Vegetable Gene Bank at Horticulture Research International (HRI), Wellesbourne in Warwickshire, seeds are dried down to 5% moisture content, hermetically sealed in foil laminate pouches, and kept at -20°C. In these conditions, their lifetime can be 30-40 years. There are of course stories of seeds lasting much longer – germinating after centuries in a Pharaoh's tomb or Aztec caves. In about 1845, for example, a certain Mr Grimstone claimed to have come into possession of some peas found in the dust of an Egyptian vase presented to the British museum by Sir Gardner Wilkinson and supposed to be 2844 years old. A few years later, Grimstone gave some seeds of the variety to the Royal Horticultural Society

for testing, but according to one early writer '...the resulting plants seemed so similar to those of Dwarf Branching Marrow that in 1849 the new-old variety was grown beside [this] well-known one, when no difference could be detected in growth, foliage, flowers, pods or seeds'! So was it just an elaborate Victorian hoax?

Germination testing

If you have plenty of seed of a particular variety, you can test its germination at any time by pregerminating a batch on paper towelling in a warm place – in an airing cupboard or propagator, for example (see p33). Count out a known number of seeds (the more you use, the more accurate your test will be), and then count the number that germinate to give you the germination rate. However, germination tests made in such conditions can be misleading. Seeds in storage tend to lose their vigour well before the seed dies completely – they may take more coaxing to germinate outside and may produce weak plants. The germination rate is best treated merely as an indication of this decline and you need to think about replenishing a batch of seed when its rate of germination is still over 60%, even though plenty of seed still appears to be viable.

Pests and diseases

Of all the diseases that can affect vegetables, relatively few are normally carried over in the seed. However, there are exceptions. Common seed-borne diseases include lettuce mosaic virus; the fungal diseases celery leaf spot and onion neck rot; and the bacterial disease halo blight which affects French and runner beans. Details of seed-borne diseases to look out for are given in the Crop-by-Crop Seed Saving chapters, but don't let them put you off. Looking at a vegetable disease book is rather like looking at a medical dictionary – you immediately discover that some minor ailment could be some rare deadly disease! Over 600 batches of home-saved seed are sent to the Heritage Seed Library each year and very few show any signs of disease.

To minimise problems, make it a general rule never to save seed from diseased or otherwise unhealthy looking plants. If all the plants are affected and you have no other batches of seed of the variety, collect the seed but mark it clearly, and don't give any away to other gardeners. Try growing it again in a different spot the following year. Don't soak or pregerminate the seeds together as this can pass on infection, and space out the plants well. With any luck, you might find that the previous year's growing conditions are responsible for the problem, or that you have at least some healthy plants to carry on the strain.

Whereas relatively few plant diseases are seed borne, many more are carried over in other forms of plant material. Soil-borne fungal diseases such as clubroot can be carried on roots, for example, and virus diseases are transmitted in tubers, cuttings and offsets. It is therefore much more difficult to maintain healthy stocks of plants 'vegetatively' propagated in this way. Nevertheless, many gardeners do save and pass on shallot sets and Jerusalem artichoke tubers for many years without any apparent problem. The Stafford Red shallot, for example, was known to have been grown on an old allotment site in the town over 60 years ago. Distinguished by the burnished red of its outer papery coat, it was passed on from allotment holder to allotment holder and from allotment to allotment, and still yields healthy crops today.

Potatoes are an exception in that they are very prone to virus diseases and usually become weak and sickly if they are home-saved for more than three or four years. Most 'seed' potatoes that you buy are grown in areas such as north east Scotland and Northern Ireland where the aphids that carry the viruses are not prevalent, and production is strictly regulated. There is a Commonwealth Potato Collection at the Scottish Crops Research Institute in Dundee which holds a large number of varieties of potato for plant breeding, and several Scottish nurseries have extensive collections of both new and old varieties that are available to gardeners. Viruses can be eliminated from potato varieties by micropropagation, but this is a laboratory process which needs special facilities. For these reasons, potatoes are not held by the Heritage Seed Library or covered in this book.

F1 hybrids

An F1 hybrid vegetable variety will not breed true – that is, if you save seed from it, these seeds will not give plants that have the same characteristics as the parent. This is because F1 hybrid seed is obtained by crossing two different parent varieties, both of which contribute genetically.

The hybrid ornamental perennials familiar as garden plants are obtained in a similar way, but there is one significant difference: once a hybrid tulip has been created, for example, the new variety is propagated vegetatively by division of the bulbs. When a vegetable hybrid has been bred, the two parent varieties which produce it must be crossed **every time** seed is needed.

Commercial seed companies producing seed of an F1 hybrid have to maintain the two parent varieties (which are inbred to make them uniform); they have to make sure that the flowers of the two varieties are ready at the same time to make the cross; and they also have to prevent self-pollination in the parent from which the F1 seed is being harvested. It is thus easy to seed why F1 seed is more expensive.

For commercial growers, F1 hybrids have two main advantages over 'open-pollinated' (i.e. non-hybrid) varieties. First, they are often more vigorous and can give higher yields; second they are more uniform in size and shape, and in the time that they are ready for harvest. However, these qualities are not always so useful to gardeners. For the seed company, one of the main advantages of developing F1 hybrids is that, because it maintains the parent varieties, only it can produce the seed.

*Audrey Adcock with seed pods of her local Sidborough strain
of Ragged Jack Kale.*

Crop-by-crop seed saving

The following chapters give guidelines on how to save seed from individual vegetable crops, and on the choice of varieties still around – whether it be in mainstream catalogues or heritage collections, or home-saved by gardeners.

For each crop it is useful to look first at what distinguishes one variety from another: factors such as physical appearance, harvest time, and resistance to disease. This is less obvious than you might think, and seed catalogues rarely give the whole picture. French bean varieties, for example, are most likely to be described by the shape and colour of their pods. However, their flowers can also vary widely in colour from dark purple through various shades of lilac and pink to pure white. Although this doesn't affect how you grow them or eat them, it is important if you are roguing a crop for seed saving, or looking for a particular old variety, or even if you are planning an ornamental kitchen garden. Sometimes varieties with one particular characteristic have become so dominant in shops and seed catalogues that you may not realise that others exist: that there are orange beetroot as well as purple ones, for example.

It is also useful to put crops in a historical context – to know when they were first grown, which types appeared in early seed lists, and what contemporary gardening writers said about them – and to understand what modern plant breeders have done. You can then see how their diversity has been swayed by Victorian market gardeners, wartime austerity, and modern production methods, and you will know what qualities to look out for in traditional varieties that you find today. Some crops, such as peas, have been grown in Europe for centuries and the number of types in old catalogues far exceeds those available now. Others, such as tomatoes, are relative newcomers from abroad and early gardeners worked with a limited selection: in this case home seedsavers as well as modern plant breeders have since looked back to the crop's

American homeland where more diversity still exists. Whatever the crop, individual examples have been chosen to show that you can still find varieties with an interesting history, or local character, or particular qualities unmatched by those widely grown today.

It is not easy to get authoritative guidance on garden seed saving. Most of the available literature is aimed either at large scale commercial seed producers (nearly all of whom are abroad) or at American gardeners. The last official guidelines for UK commercial seed growers were published 40 or 50 years ago by the National Institute of Agricultural Botany. Most of the practical advice given in the following chapters therefore comes from the staff at the Heritage Seed Library and from gardeners who save seed for themselves. As well as members who can obtain varieties from a yearly catalogue, the Heritage Seed Library has 'Seed Guardians' who agree to raise seed of a chosen variety for the Library and to fill in a report form about it. The Seed Search had extra seedsavers who similarly grew and reported on varieties sent to the project. In addition, the gardeners at HDRA's Ryton, Audley End and Yalding Organic Gardens also grow many traditional varieties and save seed. It is the experiences of all these different gardeners, growing different varieties in different conditions – and using the produce in different ways – that makes the advice so pertinent and the tips so valuable.

Beetroot, spinach beet and chard

Species: *Beta vulgaris*
Family: *CHENOPODIACEAE*

Beetroot, spinach beet and chard are all derived from the wild plant *Beta vulgaris*, but over the centuries they have been selected for different characteristics – beetroot for the shape and colour of its roots, spinach beet for its large leaves, and chard for its thick midribs – so that the types now appear quite distinct. However, they are all the same species and will readily cross-pollinate.

For beetroot, the shape and colour of the roots are the main characteristics which distinguish different varieties. The roots can be globe shaped, flattened, conical or cylindrical, and although most are red or purple in colour, they can be yellow or white. The earliest catalogues simply list 'beets: red, white or green', and whether these are used for leaf or root is not made clear. By the end of the 19th century, however, many different named red beetroot and several yellow ones were on offer to gardeners. The long conical rooted types which had most of the root in the ground were a type mostly used for winter storage, whereas the flat 'turnip-rooted' types sat mostly above the ground and were hence said to be good for growing on clay soils. There were many local strains: 'Dark crimson coloured Beets are those which are most esteemed by market gardeners, most of whom grow their seeds saved from selected plants' said William Robinson in 1885.

The leaves of beetroot can also be very distinctive, and in Victorian times the crop was popular as a hardy, easy to grow foliage plant for summer displays. Specific varieties were sold for this purpose, mostly selected for their rich dark, sometimes wavy edged foliage, although the roots were edible too. In the 1880s Sutton's listed a

McGregor's Favourite

variety called Sutton's Bedding, for example, and as late as the 1930s Carters listed the variety Flower Garden. Unfortunately most of these ornamental varieties have now disappeared, although two – Bulls Blood and Mr McGregor's Favourite – can still be found.

Much of the beetroot grown commercially today is used for processing, which usually means precooking and dousing in vinegar. For this varieties need to be easy to slice, like the cylindrical types, or they must produce uniform baby beets; most of the varieties in today's catalogues are small globe-shaped beets, and they increasingly include F1 hybrids. The roots must also be a good red colour throughout with no off-colour rings. Gardeners, however, may want large roots – good for winter storage – or ones which have a different coloured flesh. They will almost certainly be interested in the taste of the beets when used fresh – perhaps raw in salads or baked in the oven – and this varies considerably between varieties. They may also want to get the best value for space by using the beetroot's edible leaves.

The 'seeds' of beetroot that you buy are actually corky fruits or seed clusters, which normally contain anything between two and four seeds. However, plant breeders have recently produced 'monogerm' varieties where the fruits each contain only one seed, and if these are spaced carefully when sowing, no subsequent thinning is necessary. Although this can save a lot of time and money for commercial growers with fields full of beetroot, it is rarely of much importance to gardeners.

With spinach beet and chard, it is obviously the characteristics of the leaves rather than the roots that are significant: these vary between varieties in size and curliness and in the width and colour of the leafstalk. 'Rainbow chard' with a mixture of coloured stems has recently been offered by catalogues but it is not new: varieties with bright red and deep yellow leafstalks were grown in Victorian times, although more as an ornamental plant than as a vegetable.

One important characteristic for all these crops is resistance to bolting: they are all biennials and should not run to seed in their first summer. If this does happen, a cold snap after the seedlings have emerged is the most likely cause, but hot dry conditions and poor soils can also be a trigger. Some varieties are more resistant to bolting then others.

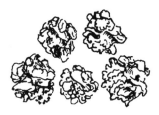

Beetroot seed clusters

Saving seed of beetroot

Beetroot are popular with home seed savers, even though they are biennial and the roots or plants have to be kept overwinter. However, sometimes cross-pollination can be a problem.

Growing and roguing

Producing seed from overwintered roots

In the first year, grow the beetroot just as you would for the kitchen, sowing in time to get reasonably large well-shaped roots for winter storage. Beetroot respond well to sowing in modules and transplanting (p33), so use this method to give them a good start if necessary. As the plants grow, remove any that bolt or which look unhealthy or not true to type – look at the shape, colour and coarseness of the leaves. Some virus and other diseases that show leaf symptoms can be carried over in the seed.

Lift the roots in autumn and select the best – with shape, size and colour typical of the variety – for seed saving. As beetroot are outbreeders, you should select and keep as many as you can in order to preserve the health and genetic diversity of the variety (p42) – ideally at least 16. In mild areas or in polytunnels, you could leave the plants in the ground over winter, but in most cases you will need to store them in damp sand or leafmould in a cool frost-free place.

Set the roots out in spring, as soon as danger of severe frost has passed. Plant them firmly, in blocks or rows, with roots at least 30cm apart and with their crown at soil level. When leaves and flower stems appear, remove any plants that do not look healthy.

Producing seed from overwintered plants

An alternative method is to overwinter young plants rather than mature roots. Sow the seed much later (late August in central England), overwinter the plants with protection – either in the border of a greenhouse or tunnel, under cloches, or in pots. At the Heritage Seed Library, three seedlings are grown in 20cm pots and kept in a polytunnel over winter; then planted out as before in early spring. This is a useful method if you find roots difficult to store over winter and re-establish in spring, but it does not give such good opportunities for roguing and selection.

Pollination and isolation

Beetroot will cross pollinate not only with other beetroot varieties, but with spinach beet and chards, and also with agricultural fodder and sugar beets. If you are saving seed you need to know whether other varieties or types of beet are likely to be flowering nearby. The pollen is wind-borne and can travel over relatively long distances, so the isolation distances recommended to commercial seed growers are large: a minimum of 500m for similar varieties (e.g. between two globe-shaped beetroot) and anything from 1-3km for different types of crop (e.g. between beetroot and sugar beet).

However, if you are not near any agricultural crops and only grow one variety for seed, you may not need to worry about cross-pollination. Crops grown just for eating should not be a threat, provided any bolters are removed before they flower. Cages covered with insect-proof mesh may not be satisfactory for isolating beets, as the pollen is fine enough to pass through even a very small mesh. However, they should reduce the airflow and the probability of contamination – especially if other crops are some distance away. Horticultural fleece is more likely to prevent pollen entering, but can cause problems with humidity.

The tall stiffly snaking flower spikes of beetroot are surprisingly attractive: '[They] looked amazing and smelt delightful – like honey' said Seed Guardian Jane Gifford from Co. Durham. In his book *Jitterbug Perfume*, American author Tom Robbins even makes beet flowers the elusive ingredient of a perfume that allows his characters to live for hundreds of years! The spikes are much branched and can grow to 1m or more; they will usually need staking.

Harvesting and cleaning seed

The seeds are mature when the 'fruits' or seed clusters turn brown, which they do successively from the base of the flower spike upwards. However, they do not fall off readily, so if the weather conditions are good they can be left on the plant until all of them are ripe. Otherwise cut off whole flower spikes when the bottom seeds are mature and brown, and hang them up in a warm airy place to finish drying. Pinch off the tips of the stalks where the seed clusters are small and immature. The mature dry clusters can then easily be stripped from the stalks by hand, but you may need to wear gloves as they are rough and hard. Sieve to remove any debris and dust.

Saving seed of spinach beet and chard

These crops are saved for seed in exactly the same way as beetroot, except that the plants are left in the ground overwinter. Cover chard plants with cloches in periods of severe weather as they are not always winter hardy.

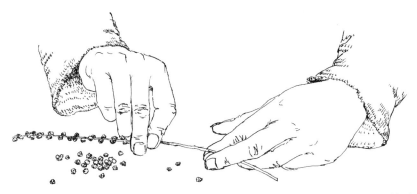

Stripping beetroot seed by hand

Varieties

Some traditional varieties survive in modern catalogues, including the standard favourite Detroit Globe, which dates back at least to the early 1900s. You can also find (but only just...) varieties with different coloured roots; these can look attractive in salads and don't make the chopping board, your fingers, or the rest of the ingredients a vivid pink! The commonest ones are: the yellow-fleshed **Burpee's Golden**; the white **Albina Vereduna**, said to be a Dutch heirloom variety with a very sweet flavour, and the Italian **Barbabietola di Chioggia** which inside has rings of alternate red and white. The Heritage Seed Library collection includes a few family heirloom beetroot and some old commercial varieties popular with home seedsavers.

Devoy

A variety with long tapering roots which keeps its tenderness and flavour even when allowed to grow large. Heritage Seed Library member Phyllis Tonbell said she had to 'top and tail' hers just to get them in the pan! A good variety for winter storage. It was originally donated to the Heritage Seed Library by John Coutts of Aberdeen Allotments and Gardens Society who said 'It has been in my friend's family for two generations and has often been a winner on the show bench'.

Bulls Blood

An old variety renowned for its decorative reddish-purple leaves, which are broad with a distinctly wavy edge. However, its round medium-sized roots are still good for eating, as reports from Heritage Seed Library members over the years confirm, and it is one of the most popular varieties in the collection. Seed Guardian Jackie Warner says 'They store and cook well giving a lovely light claret-looking flesh. The flavour is truly excellent'. Mary Rickards from Shropshire sells the variety to the Italian chef at

Bulls Blood

a local restaurant who uses the leaves as a chard because of their stunning colour.

Avonearly

Bred from the old Detroit types of beetroot by the then National Vegetable Research Station (now HRI) at Wellesbourne in Warwickshire, with the aim of producing a variety with good resistance to bolting. It is thus ideal for early sowings to give small tender beet. Its globe-shaped roots are deep red throughout, almost free of lighter coloured rings. A popular variety with gardeners for years, it remained on the National List until the late 1990s and has since been maintained by the Heritage Seed Library.

Cheltenham Green Top

This variety has long medium-sized roots with a broad shoulder and, quite the opposite to the decorative beets, has deep green leaves. It is good for winter storage. A correspondent to the *Gardeners' Chronicle* in 1889 praises its quality '..Messr's Veitch & Sons and Messr's Harrison & Sons showed ...a kind called Cheltenham Green Top...This is a valuable variety of beet, and scarcely any other is grown in the market gardens around Cheltenham.' This praise is borne out by the fact that over 100 years later, the variety is still in the seed catalogues.

McGregor's Favourite

One of the few decorative varieties to remain in current seed catalogues – look for it in the Flower Garden sections where the constraints of the National List never applied. It has narrow shimmering reddish bronze foliage which springs out neatly from the crown, and small stumpy roots. The variety is said to have originated in Scotland, certainly by the 1920s (probably earlier), but the identity of Mr McGregor appears a mystery.

Cook's Delight

This variety has long elongated oval roots and striking burgundy red leaves, appreciated by some Heritage Seed Library members for both their ornamental and edible value. Guardian Martin Hyde recommends that the roots are best harvested small. It is probably similar to the variety Cylindra which is still available, although both were tested separately in National Institute of Agricultural Botany trials in 1976 and the name 'Cook's Delight' is much more evocative ... presumably it is a 'delight' because it produces even slices when cut?

Broad bean

Species: *Vicia faba*
Family: *LEGUMINOSAE*

One broad bean may seem much like another, but if you know what to look for there are surprising differences between them. The eating quality of a variety is generally considered to depend mainly on the size and skin-colour of the fresh bean. However, if you use broad beans as whole young pods (delicious steamed and tossed in olive oil!), or if you let them grow large and then skin and puree the beans themselves, you may be looking for slightly different characteristics. To gardeners, the hardiness and height of the plants, and when they crop are also important.

The beans grown in medieval times were probably small-seeded types like the 'field' or 'tic' beans grown for stock today. However, the earliest 17th and 18th century seed lists already contain large-seeded 'Windsor' beans, and the 1831 report on broad beans cultivated in the gardens of the Horticultural Society listed 11 distinct types. There were large-seeded varieties and small-seeded ones, and as well as green and white-seeded types, there were those with red or purple seeds. Some were tall and some dwarf, and the colour of the flowers varied from pure white to dark crimson. The collection must have shown much more variation than you will find in similar garden trials today.

By late Victorian times, gardeners had begun to favour the large-seeded 'longpod' beans over the small-seeded types for early sowings, and then often used Windsor types for the main crop. Longpods typically have longer, thinner pods containing more, slightly smaller seeds, and the plants are generally hardier. Windsors are characterised by short broad pods containing only about three large seeds. They have always had a reputation for flavour: 'For the epicures and others that are fastidious in respect of quality, there is the section of Windsor beans – large, tender, full of flavour, and, when well managed, as green as grass when put upon the table.' said one gardening writer in 1884.

Today many broad beans are still classified as Windsors or longpods, although there are lots of intermediate types. Some mainstream catalogues also now offer small-seeded varieties that have pure white flowers (with no black splotch); these have recently been bred for processing, but are marketed to gardeners as the broad bean equivalent of 'petit pois'.

Saving seed

Broad beans are usually easy to grow for seed – the pods mature early and the seeds are easy to collect. However, cross-pollination between varieties can be a great problem and it is often difficult to keep varieties true to type.

Growing and roguing

Start the beans just as you would for an edible crop, sowing at the normal time: usually early spring unless you are sure the variety will overwinter from autumn sowing. Early sowing is preferable because the plants will grow best in the cool conditions early in the season, and it gives plenty of time for the seeds to mature and dry in late summer. The seed can be pre-germinated and/or sown in pots if necessary (p33). Late-sown crops are more likely to suffer from blackfly, and from diseases such as rust and chocolate spot which can be carried over in the seed.

As broad beans are outbreeders, try to grow as many plants as you can for seed saving – ideally a minimum of 24. This helps to maintain the health and diversity of the variety (p42) and gives you plenty of leeway for roguing and selection. Space the plants 20cm apart each way in a double row, or 30cm apart each way in a block. Tall varieties will almost always need staking. Before flowering starts, remove any plants that look unhealthy or that are very different to the rest in height or habit. Leaves puckered and/or patterned with a yellow or green mosaic are signs of virus disease.

Pollination and isolation

Broad beans will readily cross-pollinate with other broad bean varieties (and with any field beans growing nearby), the pollen being carried by bees. To keep seed saving simple, you really need to have an isolated plot and grow only one variety both for eating and for seed.

Commercially seed crops of broad beans are grown a minimum of 1000m apart, but in a garden with plenty of living barriers much smaller distances should give acceptable results. It also helps if you can grow a large number of plants, set out in a block rather than rows. Experiments with field beans have shown that, for example, you could expect only a very small percentage of crossing to occur in a 4.5m[2] plot of beans grown 25m from another variety. Seed saved only from plants at the centre of this block would be even purer (p37). Of course, for this you need plenty of space and seed, but it can be worth it to get pure seed, and a large plot of beans in flower looks and smells wonderful – it was even enough to inspire poet John Clare, whose love was '...as sweet as a bean field in blossom'!

Physical barriers are not usually recommended for isolating broad beans in the garden, because to get a good set and maintain the variety in the long term, pollen must be transferred between the flowers by bees. Some of the flowers of broad beans will usually self-pollinate, and a proportion of pods will usually set if the plants are physically isolated, but the mechanisms involved in this are quite complex. You cannot go on isolating plants in subsequent generations without drastically affecting the pod set and the health of the variety.

Selection and harvesting and cleaning seed

When the plants start to flower, check the flower colour and remove any plants that are not true to type immediately. When they start to pod, check the shape and length of the pods and choose the best ones, most typical of the variety, for seed saving. Mark them clearly if you are also picking for eating. Frank Clark who has been saving his family heirloom variety for over 50 years (p7), keeps seed from only the first two sets of pods on each of the plants he selects; the rest are used for the kitchen. 'Being the earliest to form' he says 'they have maximum growth time to produce the best quality seed for the following season.'

If possible, leave the pods on the plant in the garden to dry. However, once the seeds are mature and the pods start to lose their colour and springiness, whole plants can be pulled up if necessary and brought into a warm airy place to dry (p44). Small quantities of seed can then easily be separated by hand podding, and dried further if they need it until ready for storage.

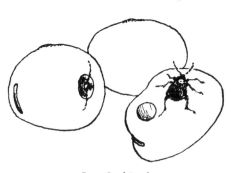

Bean Seed Beetle

Remove any that are discoloured or badly damaged. Neat circular holes about 1-2mm in diameter will usually have been caused by the larvae of the bean seed beetle. The immature larvae burrow into the developing seeds in the pod; here they pupate, and emerge as adults when the seed matures. They will often have disappeared by the time you pod the beans for seed, but not always – sometimes you will see a head and antennae peeping from one of the holes! Although the holes look unsightly and can make the seed unsuitable for passing on to other gardeners, in fact they do not usually cause sufficient damage to affect germination. It is sometimes suggested that the seeds are put in the freezer to kill any beetles or larvae remaining. If you do this, make sure the seeds are thoroughly dry otherwise they can be damaged by the freezing process. Even if you don't, there is no danger that the beetles will affect more of the seeds in store as they need the growing plants to go on and complete their life-cycle.

Varieties

Several very old varieties, or modern selections of them, are relatively widely available: the green-seeded variety **Green Windsor**, for example, which appeared in seed lists and literature in the early 1800s, and **White Windsor** which was probably grown very much earlier. **Aquadulce Claudia**, still justifiably recommended as one of the hardiest varieties for autumn sowing, was introduced from the continent in the later half of the nineteenth century, and the longpod variety **Bunyard's Exhibition** probably dates back to before 1900.

Gardeners often saved their own seeds of broad beans in the past, and many of the home-saved varieties and family heirlooms that have survived are selected strains of Windsors or longpods. However, some – such as the Heritage Seed Library's Martock bean – are closer to field beans. Other varieties have been kept in cultivation for the colour of their seeds or – like the stunningly beautiful Crimson-flowered – for the colour of their blooms.

Bowland's Beauty

A home-saved longpod variety that has been carefully grown and selected over the years for just that – its long pods. Yorkshire farm worker George Bowland has been growing them and saving seed for nearly 40 years, having been given some at a local horticultural show by another exhibitor who was himself on the point of retirement. It is a tall, white-seeded variety which produces a heavy crop of pods that are usually 30cm or more in length. Jennifer Russell from Osmotherley who sent the seeds to the Seed Search project (p24) says she gets beans 35cm or more long. A novice to vegetable growing, she began to realise just how good they were when she joined the local gardening club and entered their show: 'I began winning prizes' she says 'not only to my own amazement but to others as well!'.

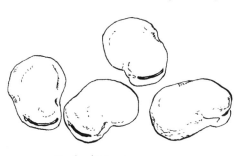

Bowland's Beauty

Red Epicure

A long-pod type of bean, bred by Unwins over 50 years ago, distinctive for its deep chestnut crimson seeds. The beans start to redden as they approach the edible stage and, according to Unwins, keep their colour if cooked in a steamer. A tall variety with pods which usually contain around four to five beans. Much missed by gardeners in years when it did not appear in Unwins catalogue: 'The beans were the best I have ever tasted', said Michael Drew from Norfolk, bemoaning the fact that he had not been able to find seed of the variety that year. However, the variety is still on the National List.

Crimson-flowered broad bean

Broad beans with red or crimson flowers are mentioned in early horticultural literature. They were described in British gardening books in the early 1800s, but they appear never to have been widely grown. Certainly it was a surprise when seeds of a home-saved strain arrived at HDRA back in the late 1970s. They were sent by an elderly lady, Miss Rhoda Cutbush from Harrietsham in Kent, whose father had grown the beans in the vegetable plot on the family's farm. He had originally obtained the seeds back in the 1920s from a cottager in the nearby village of Platt's Heath. After Mr Cutbush was no longer able to garden, Rhoda and her sister Nora grew the beans, and despite moving house and garden several times, managed to keep the variety alive. It has been enjoyed by thousands of Heritage Seed Library members since, both for its beautiful crimson flowers and for eating. The plants are hardy and sturdy – many report success with autumn sowings – and produce a large number of pods each containing a few medium-sized beans. 'Quite magnificent' says Peter Berrisford from Staffordshire 'They cook wonderfully and remain bright green on the plate.'

Martock

Back in 1976, Reverend Peter Coney from the small village of Martock in Somerset offered samples of these seeds to those making donations to the village church restoration find. Reverend Coney obtained his supply of beans from a local farm where they had been grown 'for time out of mind', and he found references to similar beans in Martock's manorial accounts, the earliest being in 1293-4. Steve Oxbrow, who sent some of the seeds to HDRA, likes to think this small-seeded bean really is a medieval relic – it could certainly be closely related. The variety has sturdy plants which produce purple tinted flowers and clusters of upward-pointing pods typical of a field bean. However, many Heritage Seed Library members over the years have found the beans good to eat – mealy but not at all bitter. The dry beans are mahogany brown.

Gloster Bounty

A sturdy dwarf variety growing to about 60-70cm tall, popular with Heritage Seed Library members for windy plots. The plants produce well-filled pods of five to six white-skinned beans. Long time Seed Guardian Martin Hyde from Stonehouse in Gloucestershire finds it an excellent broad bean, although not always frost hardy so best for spring sowings. Anne St John from Perthshire says 'The plants are trouble free and a pleasure to have in the garden. It's a hard discipline to keep plenty of seed – I'd like to eat the lot!'

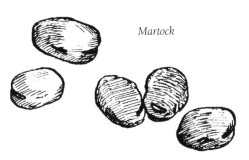

Martock

Carrot

Species: *Daucus carota*
Family: *UMBELLIFERAE*

Carrot varieties are traditionally grouped according to the time they take to mature, and by the shape of their roots. 'Early' carrots mature quickly; 'maincrop' varieties take longer and are usually left to grow larger. Within the two groups, root shapes can vary enormously from small and round to large and stumpy or long and tapering. Round or stumpy types are the best on poor soils, whereas those with long tapering roots only do well on deep sandy soils, or on the specially prepared beds used to grow carrots for show.

The flavour of a carrot will depend to some extent on variety: some are sweet, some bland, whilst others have a more distinct carrot flavour – given to them by the volatile compounds called 'terpenoids' which they contain in varying amounts. However, flavour also depends on growing conditions. Too much water and not enough light gives the tasteless carrots all too often found on the supermarket shelves. Another distinct characteristic of a variety can be the amount and vigour of the foliage. Many traditional maincrop varieties have lots of strong tall leaves which help to suppress weeds, and can also look attractive in flower beds and potagers.

Although bright orange is the colour that leaps from the carrot pages of modern seed catalogues, it is only the plant breeders that have made it that way. The first carrots to be grown in Europe came from Arab countries in about the thirteenth or fourteenth centuries. The initial ones were purple or 'red', and these were followed by a yellow type which grew mostly above ground. Orange carrots were only developed from these types in the Netherlands during the seventeenth century, but soon largely replaced them. So in the 1670s, colour was the main distinguishing feature of the 'red', 'orange' or 'yellow' carrots offered by seedsman William Lucas. Even in Victorian times, several varieties of white and yellow carrots appear in catalogues along with the orange ones, which by then were offered in a great range of shapes, sizes, and maturity times.

The kitchen gardeners for Victorian country estates were expected to produce a continual supply of small young carrots: they used hot beds and frames and made successional sowings of varieties such as French Forcing and Scarlet Horn. These varieties provided the '...elegant and delicate roots that appear on the table where the cottager's carrots dare not be seen'. In such households, the cooks frequently used the larger maincrop carrots in soups, or cut into shapes and glazed for garnishing, or for making sweet carrot puddings and tarts. The juice of the dark orange carrots was also used to colour butter.

Since then, it is orange carrots that have been almost exclusively grown in Europe, with plant breeders concentrating on improving their yield, shape and colour. However, in Asia – particularly Afghanistan – purple-rooted carrots may still be found in cultivation. Nearly all new carrot varieties bred today are F1 hybrids, usually with medium-sized cylindrical roots of a deep orange colour. These give commercial growers more reliable seed and more uniform roots, but although they are appearing in increasing numbers in home seed catalogues, most offer little advantage over open-pollinated varieties to gardeners. A few have been bred that have some resistance to carrot root fly.

Saving seed

Carrots are biennial, so to save seed you must overwinter roots or plants. In their second year they produce spectacular 'umbels' made up of many tiny flowers. These are usually a frothy white, and they attract numerous bees and hoverflies.

These flowers will cross-pollinate with any other variety of carrot that is in flower, so it is easiest just to grow one variety for seed each year. Carrots grown to eat are not a problem, provided that any roots that bolt in their first year are pulled out before they flower. Commercial seed growers isolate flowering carrot varieties by at least 1000m.

Unfortunately cultivated carrots will also cross with the wild carrot (also *Daucus carota*) which is a common wild flower in grassy places. You need to check in advance whether this plant is growing nearby. In summer it is easily distinguished by the fine forked bracts beneath the white flower umbels. If you are in an area with wild

Carrot flower

carrot, or want to grow more than one variety for seed, you will have to physically isolate your plants while they are in flower.

Growing and roguing

Producing seed from overwintered roots

Sow the seed at the normal time for maincrop carrots in your area – May/June in central England. To make the most of a very small amount of seed, carrots can be sown singly in modules provided they are planted out quickly before the tap roots start to develop. Grow the plants on as you would for a crop grown to eat. Keep the plants under fleece or fine mesh if your carrots are normally attacked by carrot root fly, as damaged roots will not usually overwinter. Remove any plants that bolt, or that have foliage that looks unhealthy or very different from the rest. Reddening stunted foliage may be a symptom of carrot motley dwarf virus, which can be carried over in the seed.

In mid-late autumn, lift the roots. Put aside for eating any that are damaged, misshapen, off-colour or otherwise very different to the rest, and for seed saving pick out those whose size, colour and shape best match the characteristics of the variety. Heritage Seed Library member John Purves, who developed his own strain of purple carrots (see p72), emphasises the importance of this: 'As with all self-saved seed,' he says 'there is the need to continually select out only the most true-to-type for growing on.'

To preserve the genetic variation and health of the variety, you should try to end up with at least 16 roots from which to save seed. Trim the foliage from the roots and store them in a box of moist leafmould or coir in a cool frost-free and rodent-free place. Replant them in early spring. Alternatively, in mild areas on sandy well-drained soil, you could replant the roots immediately and cover them with straw in severe weather.

When replanting, make sure the roots are well firmed in, with the crown at or just below the soil surface. Space them about 45cm apart in a row or block. Block planting is usually easier if you are going to physically isolate the plants later.

Producing seed from overwintered plants

An alternative to this method is to overwinter relatively young plants, sowing the seed in late summer and giving them protection in winter if neccessary. At the Heritage Seed Library, carrots are sometimes overwintered in pots as with beetroot. This method may be preferable if you have problems overwintering mature roots and re-establishing them, but it has the disadvantage that there is less opportunity to assess and rogue the roots.

Isolation and pollination

The flower stalks produced by the overwintered plants by early/mid summer can be tall – up to 1.5m or more – and usually need staking. If there are likely to be other flowering carrots or wild carrots nearby, you will need to isolate your plants by covering them with fleece or a mesh cage before the flowers open (p 38-40). The small carrot flowers that make up each umbel open progressively, from the outer whorl to the centre, over a long period. They do not self-pollinate – usually insects move pollen from flower to flower, and from umbel to umbel on both the same and different plants. For caged plants, blowflies can be introduced into the cages to carry out the pollination, and this is the method used at the Heritage Seed Library. An alternative sometimes recommended is to try hand pollination, which involves stroking the heads with a soft-haired brush every day whilst the flowers on it are still opening. You could do this with caged plants or by bagging lots of individual flowerheads. However, you must move the brush from head to head and transfer pollen between different plants, whilst at the same time prevent insects from landing on the flowers.

Collecting, drying and cleaning seed

The seed is ripe when it turns brown and the umbels become brittle. This happens over a period of several weeks, with seed on the top 'primary' umbels ripening first. Check the seedheads regularly and if possible harvest the seed from each one as it becomes ready by gently rubbing off the dry ripe seeds into a paper bag. If conditions are poor, all the stems can be cut at this stage and brought into a dry warm airy place (p 44). By then, a good proportion of seeds will be mature enough to continue to ripen indoors. When the heads are thoroughly dry and brittle, rub the seed off by hand as before or use scissors to snip them off with the very ends of the stems.

Carrot seed

Research has shown that seed from the primary umbels of carrots generally germinates more quickly and gives more vigorous seedlings, so if you have plenty of plants and only need a limited quantity of seed, it is better to collect seed from these umbels rather than collect all the seed from just a few plants.

At the Heritage Seed Library, a series of sieves are often used to separate the seed from the chaff, although you may be able to get rid of fine particles by winnowing. Carrot seeds are covered in fine spines (through a hand lens they look like little hairy insects!), and this can make them quite difficult to clean. In commercial seed-cleaning processes the spines are removed, but this is not necessary for home-saved seed. Nevertheless, some spines can be rubbed off when you are sieving seed, and you should always wear a dust mask to prevent inhaling them.

Varieties

Despite the proliferation of new varieties and F1 hybrids, several old garden favourites such as **Amsterdam Forcing** and **Autumn King** – both of which date back to at least the 1930s are still readily available, and the Victorian varieties **Long Red Surrey** and

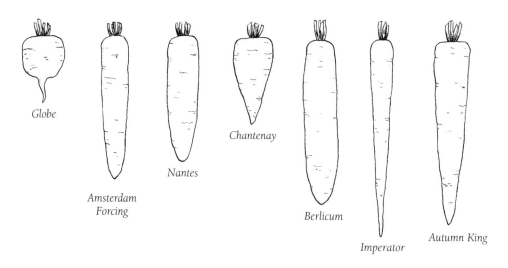

Globe

Amsterdam
Forcing

Nantes

Chantenay

Berlicum

Imperator

Autumn King

James Scarlet Intermediate (see below) can be found in some catalogues. Others, along with some more unusual types, are in the Heritage Seed Library. Few gardeners seem to save carrots for seed and home-saved strains are rare.

Altringham

A very long slender variety with little core, widely grown on a field scale in the 19th century. It appears in the seed list of one London seedsman in the 1830s, and in the 1880s is still being praised for its 'good quality and great productiveness'. The variety '... is said to have originated about 60 years ago at Altringham, a village in the vicinity of Chester' says one writer in 1876 '...In shape it is cylindrical at the upper end, tapering to a point at the lower end ...The flesh is of the first quality, deeply coloured and almost without any fibres'. This variety was one of the carrots much used for colouring butter before the discovery of annatto. The variety is not on the National List, but has been maintained by the Heritage Seed Library. It certainly produces impressive carrots on light sandy soil.

John's Purple

By selection over many years, John Purves of Oxford managed to obtained this line of purple carrots from four he found amongst a bag of orange carrots given to him by his neighbour for his rabbits. One year he passed on a batch of his seeds to the national Vegetable Gene Bank at HRI Wellesbourne and, with John's consent, they passed some to the Heritage Seed Library. As it turned out this was lucky, because developers had meanwhile taken over the site of John's allotment with the result that he had lost his carrot. When, more recently, he had space to grow it again, he was able to get seed back from the Library. The carrots have long tapering roots which are deep reddish purple in colour, and dark green leaves less finely cut than most carrot foliage. Despite the colour, which is nothing like that of a 'normal' carrot, the roots have the same distinctive carroty smell and taste.

Oxheart

In contrast to Altringham's delicate shape, this is a large chunky carrot. It is described in 1885 as being quick growing and very suitable for market garden culture: '...a thick carrot, 5 or 6 inches long...not coreless but it is still a tender and well-flavoured variety.' Over 100 years later, Heritage Seed Library Guardian Martin Hyde more or less confirms this view of the variety: '...not the prettiest you have ever seen perhaps – but wait until you taste it! An excellent flavoured carrot.'

White Belgium

One of two or three named varieties of white carrot to appear in Victorian seed lists. This one was mainly an agricultural variety because of its high yields and ability to grow in most soils. 'There is hardly a farm on which it is not grown' says Vilmorin in 1885. Nevertheless it makes a worthwhile vegetable for the kitchen. Organic grower and writer Michael Michaud, an expert on unusual vegetables, says it has 'a surprisingly good flavour', and suggests serving up a 'two carrot soup' with swirls of orange and white. It has thick tapering roots which thrust out of the ground, these upper portions of the root turning green. It is said to be susceptible to frost, so lift the roots in autumn or cover them with straw. Although still registered in Europe, the variety has not been readily available in the UK for years, and has been kept by the Heritage Seed Library since 1984.

James Scarlet Intermediate

A favourite garden carrot since the late 1880's '... probably the most popular and extensively grown for main crop purposes' said the *Gardeners' Chronicle* in 1887, and still available from some catalogues today. It has long, conical pointed roots and a reputation for doing well in most soils. In the 1990s, it was included in trials of carrot varieties for commercial organic growers carried out for the National Institute of Agricultural Botany (NIAB), and gave yields comparable to many of the modern ones under test. And what about the 'James' who gave the variety its name? Ray Warner who researches variety histories for his Heritage Seed Company Thomas Etty Esq. says that Mr James had a market garden in Lambeth Marsh, and he likes to think he was the same gardener who bred the James Long Keeping onion.

Celery and celeriac

Species: *Apium graveolens var. dulce, A. graveolens var. rapaceum*
Family: *UMBELLIFERAE*

Celery

The traditional English celery is a late autumn/early winter crop of 'trench' celery, which has been earthed up or put in collars to make it white and crisp. This type of celery has been largely superseded commercially and in gardens by self-blanching types with either white or green stems, which are much easier to grow. Their stems have naturally crisp flesh and few strings, and the white types spontaneously lose their green colour as they develop, so they do not need blanching before harvest. However, many gardeners feel that these cannot compete for crunch and taste with what they still consider to be 'the real thing'. Self-blanching celery varieties crop earlier but are less hardy than those of trench celery.

The earliest type of celery to be grown was a domesticated form of wild celery or 'smallage' used medicinally and as a flavouring. This was probably very similar to the leaf or soup celery available today – a small hardy plant with fine leaves and slender stems, which is still worth having in the garden as an easy-to-grow source of celery flavour. By the end of the seventeenth century, a celery with larger fleshier leaf stalks had been introduced from the continent and in the eighteenth century this 'solid celery' began appearing in seed lists, although it us unlikely to have been of the size and quality of celery today.

By Victorian times there were many types: varieties with red, pink or white stems, and both tall ones and dwarf ones. Webb's catalogue of 1888, for example, devotes a whole page to 18 varieties of celery from Coles Crystal White to Major

Clark's Red and enthusiastic growers could belong to 'celery clubs'. Dwarf types were most suitable for the early sowing, and red types the hardiest for late crops. All the varieties had to be planted in trenches and blanched, and gardening books of the time had pages of advice on planting and earthing up for providing continuous supplies throughout autumn and winter. This taxed gardeners considerably, and in the 1860s there was apparently '...more than one employer fond of having large and fine celery who would be so dissatisfied in the event of its failure that the gardener was no longer secure in his situation'.

The self-blanching type of celery possibly occurred as a chance mutation, which was then selected and further developed. It was already known by the mid 1880s, as Vilmorin describes a Golden Yellow celery whose ' ...stalks are naturally of an ivory-white colour, so that they do not require to be artificially blanched to improve their appearance', and says that this was developed in a market garden near Paris. The variety Golden Self Blanching remained the main one of this type in seed catalogues for many years. More recently, there has been a proliferation of new varieties – including ones suitable for growing commercially under glass both early and late in the year. Some have been bred for resistance to specific diseases and sometimes resistance to bolting. Many are F1 hybrids.

Celeriac

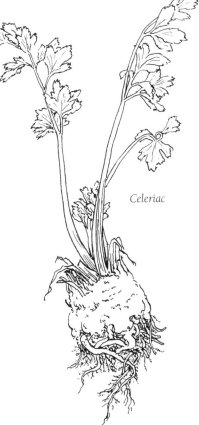

Celeriac

Celeriac, with its knobbly swollen 'bulb', cannot compete with celery as a refreshing crunchy salad but it is more than equal to it in other dishes – as a cooked vegetable in soups and stews, or grated raw in a creamy dressing – and compared with celery it is relatively easy to grow. Although it is still regarded as something of a novelty, it has been known in this country since the mid eighteenth century. It was certainly grown in some of the large Victorian kitchen gardens although, then as now, it was more widely used on the continent. Its popularity has never really increased and different named varieties rarely appeared in British seed catalogues until recently.

Today, varieties are generally bred for the size, solidity and smoothness of the 'bulb' which is made up of the swollen bases of the stems together with the upper part of the root. Breeders also aim to produce varieties whose flesh is as white as possible and does not discolour on cooking. In reality, the size and quality of the bulb depend strongly on growing conditions and it is often difficult to distinguish between different varieties from year to year in the garden.

Saving seed

Few gardeners save celery or celeriac seeds, and there is little information on maintaining varieties in the garden. However, celeriac – which is relatively easy to overwinter – should be no more difficult to save for seed than beetroot or carrot.

All the different types of celery and celeriac are biennial, and all will cross-pollinate with each other, so it is easiest just to grow one type and variety per year for seed. Other varieties grown for eating are not a problem, as long as any that bolt are removed before they flower. Celery and celeriac can also cross-pollinate with wild celery, but this is not a widely distributed wild plant, being mostly found in damp grassy places in coastal areas.

Growing and roguing

In the first year, grow the plants as you would for eating. Remove any that bolt early or do not grow vigorously, and also any whose leaves or stems look unhealthy or very different from the rest. Keep as many of the best, most true-to-type plants as you can for seed saving. You could aim for the 16 plants recommended for carrots, although because celery does not suffer as much from inbreeding depression (p12), using less may still give satisfactory results.

Leaf Celery flower

Leaf celery is hardy – you can leave the plants in the ground over winter – but other types of celery will not withstand hard frosts and nor will celeriac. They must be protected if left in the ground or must be lifted in late autumn and stored until the spring. An alternative – if you have space – is to replant them immediately into the border of a polytunnel and grow them on there until the seed is harvested.

If plants are left in the ground, pack straw around them and during short spells of severe weather cover the plants with polythene sheeting. If you opt for storage, celeriac can be treated like other root crops: trim the 'bulbs' of leaves and put them in boxes of moist sand, coir or leafmould. This also gives you a chance to examine them more carefully and choose the best, most typical ones for seed saving. Celery is less easy to store successfully: the roots need to be damp and the stems relatively dry to prevent rotting. It is sometimes recommended that plants are packed upright in boxes with their roots resting on moist sand or earth, and the boxes stored overwinter in a cool frost-free place.

Replant stored plants firmly in early spring. By early summer they will have formed branched flower spikes with umbels of tiny white flowers. The spikes can reach a height of 1m or more and will probably need staking.

Pollination and isolation

The small flowers on the umbels open successively just like those of carrots, and pollen is carried from one to another and from plant to plant by insects. If there are likely to be other celery or celeriac varieties flowering nearby, you will need to isolate your plants by covering them with a netting or fleece cage and introducing blowflies for pollination (see p38-40). Commercial seed growers isolate different varieties of celery by a distance of at least 500m.

Collecting, drying and cleaning seed

The seed is ready for harvest when the plants begin to turn yellow and most of the seeds on the main umbels have turned grey-brown in colour. Celery is notorious for shedding seed readily, so if possible harvest the seed from each umbel as it becomes ripe by gently rubbing off the dry seeds into a paper bag. If conditions are poor, all the stems can be cut onto a sheet or into a paper sack at this stage and brought into a dry warm airy place (p44).

Celery and celeriac seeds are tiny, and can be quite difficult to clean. As they are so light, winnowing is not easy and at the Heritage Seed Library they are cleaned with sieves.

Varieties

Today's garden seed catalogues rarely list more than one variety of trench celery, and many of the traditional varieties have disappeared. However, there are still a small range of them available, differing mainly in stalk colour, size, and hardiness. A few Victorian varieties such as **Solid Pink**, **Solid White** and **Giant Red** – or modern selections of them – are still listed in some catalogues, as is the once popular **Golden Self Blanching**.

Josie and Laurie help to hand pollinate Boothbys Blond cucumbers

Cucumber

Species: *Cucumis sativus*
Family: *CUCURBITACEAE*

Cucumbers are generally categorised into indoor or 'greenhouse' varieties and outdoor or 'ridge' varieties. Greenhouse cucumbers have long, smooth cylindrical green fruit – they are the sort required for tea on the vicarage lawn, and are still sometimes referred to as 'English' cucumbers. For the gardener and seed saver, an important characteristic of greenhouse cucumbers is that they are 'parthenocarpic': that is, they will produce fruit without pollination, although this fruit is naturally seedless.

Traditional ridge cucumbers, on the other hand, are short with rougher thicker skins, sometimes with warts and spines. Unlike greenhouse cucumbers, they need pollinating to produce fruit and you need to pick them young for eating, before the seeds become tough. Gherkins, which are usually even rougher, are not just immature cucumbers but are small-fruited ridge kinds, sometimes having drier flesh which makes them good for pickling.

We have the Victorians to blame – or credit – for the ubiquity of the long straight greenhouse cucumber. In the last half of the 19th century, such fruit were highly esteemed and often given a disproportionate amount of attention compared to other crops. Special low-pitched glass-houses, heated with hot water pipes were built to accommodate them, and it was said that there was 'nothing more creditable to the gardener than a good house of cucumbers'. Numerous 'improved' varieties were developed, all with the long green fruit considered desirable at the time, and all of which grew best in the steady moist heat of these custom-built houses. The characteristic of producing parthenocarpic fruit was important because under glass in winter, there were few insects for pollination. In comparison, the hardier cucumbers – some short, some white-skinned and some spiny – which were offered by earlier seedsman received scant attention.

Modern breeding has largely replaced traditional greenhouse cucumbers with 'all-female' F1 hybrid varieties, which produce similar long straight fruit and are equally fussy about growing conditions. They have the great advantage to commercial growers that no male flowers are produced: every flower produces a fruit and there can be no pollination, which can make the fruit misshapen and bitter. At the same time, breeding of ridge varieties has been aimed at making the fruit look more like greenhouse cucumbers, and the plants more compact and higher yielding. Again many are F1 hybrids. However, for gardeners, traditional varieties of both greenhouse and ridge types can crop just as well as some of the hybrids, and of course they can be saved for seed. As well as cylindrical green types, there are some ridge varieties with white or yellow skins, and ones that are round or oval, spiny or ridged. If you like your cucumbers peeled and diced in yoghurt, shredded in chilled soups, or stuffed hot or cold, then appearances are not so important as hardiness and flavour.

One of the commonest cucumber problems is powdery mildew – the dusty white coating that appears on the leaves towards the end of the season particularly in greenhouses and polytunnels. Susceptibility depends on variety, and some modern varieties have been bred to be less susceptible. Information on the disease resistance of older varieties is often lacking.

Saving seed

Cucumbers are reasonably easy to save for seed, once you have sorted out their unusual sex life, although cross-pollination can be a problem.

Growing and roguing

Grow the crop in the same way as you would for eating: plants need to be started off inside, and in cold areas you may find it better to grow even 'outdoor' ridge cucumbers with some protection so as to be sure of getting mature fruit. As the plants grow, remove any that do not look healthy; distorted leaves with yellow mottling are a sign of cucumber mosaic virus, which can be carried in the seed.

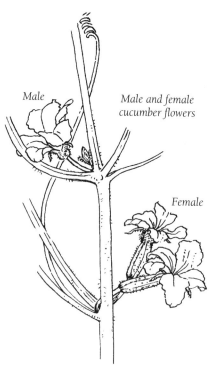

Male

Male and female cucumber flowers

Female

Pollination and isolation

Cucumbers have separate male and female flowers, both of which usually occur on the same plant at the same time. Don't worry if only male flowers appear at first, however, this is normal. Insects, particularly bees, usually carry pollen from the male flowers to the female flowers either on the same plant or on different plants. With traditional **ridge** varieties, this pollination must occur in order to obtain fruit. With traditional **greenhouse** varieties better fruit is produced without pollination, so for an edible crop this is usually prevented by picking off male flowers or excluding insects from the glasshouse (not easy!). The female flowers then produce fruit spontaneously, but this is seedless. To save seed, you must leave on some male flowers and either let insects pollinate the female flowers that are open at the same time, or bag flowers and hand pollinate them (see p41).

You can also bag and hand pollinate as a way of avoiding cross-pollination if you – or your neighbours – are growing other varieties. It is not difficult. Jill Yeates, Heritage Seed Library Guardian for the heirloom variety Boothby's Blond, gets her young son Laurie (age 5) and daughter Josie (age 11) to help her. It is a good biology lesson, and can be the best way of ensuring pure seed. Commercial seed growers are recommended to isolate different cucumber varieties by at least 1000m.

Although cucumbers are outbreeders, it does not usually seriously effect the health of the strain to inbreed them – that is, to save the seed from just one or two plants. However, it is preferable to grow more – about six if possible – and move pollen from plant to plant.

Harvesting and cleaning seed

When the fruit are at the edible stage, select and tag those which are you are going to continue to grow on for seed: they should be typical of the variety in size, shape and colour. These fruit must be allowed to ripen on the plant past the edible stage, until they begin to soften and change colour, and then you can cut them off and leave them for a few weeks in a warm dry place to finish maturing. Jill Yeates, who has saved seed from many a fruit of Boothby's Blond, advises: 'I leave the seed-fruit on the plant for as long as possible, and then leave it in a north-facing windowsill for a further three or four weeks before cutting it open.'

The colour of the mature cucumber fruit is distinctive of the variety, and may be quite different to its colour when you eat it: some varieties go yellow and some dark orange, for example. At this stage, when you slice the fruit open, the seeds and watery gel should scrape out easily into a container.

By the time the fruit has been left to mature, the gel often comes off the seed quite easily, and at the Heritage Seed Library,

Cucumber seed

seed is usually cleaned just by washing it in a sieve. However, some seedsavers find they need to ferment the seed/juice mixture. Add about an equal volume of water, and leave the mixture somewhere warm for one to two days, stirring it occasionally. A mouldy, rather smelly layer will form on the surface. At the end of this period add more water and stir. The good seeds should sink to the bottom, allowing you to carefully pour off the debris and wash the seeds as before.

Spread the clean seeds in a thin layer on a tray or plate (anything with a shiny surface so they do not stick) and put them in a warm airy place. Stir them around as they dry, to break up any clumps and help them to dry evenly. They are ready for storage when they snap in half, rather than bending.

Varieties

A few traditional Victorian greenhouse cucumbers are still listed in some catalogues, including the once widely grown commercial variety **Telegraph** (see below) and the variety **Conqueror**, said to tolerate lower temperatures than Telegraph and still popular with amateur gardeners in the 1960s. Relatively few open-pollinated ridge cucumbers are available, although you can still get a modern selection of the old favourite **Bedfordshire Prize Ridge**, and also the round, pale yellow **Crystal Apple**. This is one of the few cucumbers in the catalogues that isn't smooth, cylindrical and green, and was threatened with deletion from the National List a few years ago, so some gardeners have saved their own strains. Ridge cucumbers from Asia and Eastern Europe are also popular with home seedsavers, as in these countries a greater diversity of traditional varieties have survived. UK family heirloom cucumbers are rare.

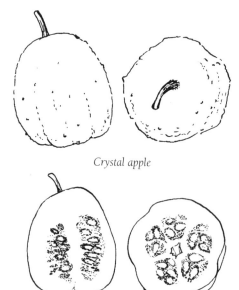

Crystal apple

Boothby's Blond

A family heirloom variety from the United States, never commercially available, which has also become popular amongst seed-savers here in its many years in the Heritage Seed Library collection. It is a traditional ridge variety needing pollination for fruit to develop. These are oval in shape, about 15cm long when ready to eat, and have a yellow warty skin covered with tufts of little black hair. 'Cut away the ugly skin' says Seed Guardian Rosemary Payne from Copthorne in Sussex, and there is '... a delightful flavour inside'. Even her husband, who doesn't normally eat cucumber likes this one.

Izjastsnoi

An old Estonian variety which was sent to the Heritage Seed Library in 1994 by Heine Refsing who runs the Danish 'Center for Bio-Diversitet', and this was one of the East European varieties the Centre was trying to keep alive. Pickled cucumbers are as much part of the East European tradition as sliced cucumber salads are of ours, so if you fancy salting and pickling, this variety seems a good one to try. However, many Heritage Seed Library members have also enjoyed it as a fresh cucumber. It is a ridge variety with many prickly green fruits on compact plants, and seems to tolerate harsh conditions well. 'Good taste, but beware of the skin' says Guardian Jeremy Garth.

Butcher's Disease Resisting

A traditional greenhouse cucumber, dating back to the early 1900s and still grown on a commercial scale in the 1960s. It is long medium green with a very smooth skin and a heavy cropper. Its importance stemmed from the fact that it was resistant to leaf spot – a cucumber disease which causes the leaves to shrivel and rot and can also spoil the fruit. You may not be likely to see the disease in your own greenhouse, but this is still a cucumber worth trying. 'Excellent flavour' says Heritage Seed Library member Mr Verney from Wales 'much preferred to any of the current all-female varieties'. Remember only to allow pollination in those fruit which you are saving for seed, as it can make them bitter.

Telegraph

A traditional greenhouse variety with long green smooth fruit introduced in the 1860s. Noted for its productiveness, as reported in the *Gardeners' Chronicle* in 1868: 'My brother gardeners who like myself are expected to produce cucumbers in quantity in the winter time should get this kind; and when they have once grown it they will not want to grow any other sort of the smooth-skinned kind.' The variety and 'improved' strains of it remained important to commercial growers until the introduction of the 'all-female' F1 hybrids. However, as yet it is still in seed catalogues for gardeners. In a trial by *Gardening Which?* in 1995, it produced as many cucumbers throughout the summer as many of the new hybrids and had equal resistance to powdery mildew. Only allow fruit you are saving for seed to pollinate, otherwise remove male flowers.

*Fred Arnold from the Isle of Wight with pods of the
dwarf French bean Brighstone.*

French bean

Species: *Phaseolus vulgaris*
Family: *LEGUMINOSAE*

Varieties of French or 'kidney' beans show an amazing variation in colour, shape and size of both the pods and seeds, and also in flower colour – much more than either runner or broad beans. They range from the polished mahogany seeds and yellow pods of some 'wax pod' beans to the bright carmine splashes of the old 'horticultural' types. In Central and South America, which are the original homelands of these beans, native Indian tribes attributed spiritual significance to the intricate patterns, and many seedsavers will empathise. 'We immediately wanted to collect a glass jar full of seed just for the joy of having them' said Paul and Leslie Gates from Derby on receiving their sample of one of the particularly beautiful heirloom beans from the Heritage Seed Library.

Other characteristics of French beans which are important for classifying them are: whether the plants are dwarf or climbing, whether they are early or late maturing, and whether or not the pods have tough 'strings' or 'parchment'. The ability to grow in cold temperatures is a also a quality worth looking for in home-saved varieties. The climber Oregon Giant and some purple-podded strains, for example, have a particular reputation for hardiness. In old catalogues, climbing French beans are often referred to as 'runners', and this adds to the confusion between these and true runner beans (*Phaseolus coccineus*) which still exists amongst some gardeners today, particularly with varieties that have been handed down rather than bought from catalogues. Runner beans usually, but not always, have much larger seeds than French beans and scarlet or white flowers. One botanical difference that distinguishes

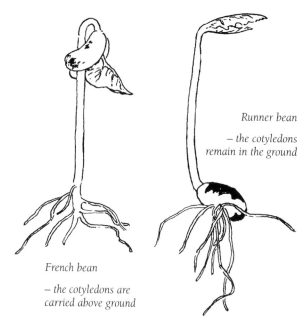

Runner bean

– the cotyledons remain in the ground

French bean

– the cotyledons are carried above ground

them easily is in the way the seedling emerges.

French bean varieties are also sometimes classified according to the uses to which they are put: the pods may be eaten as a fresh vegetable; the beans inside may be shelled and cooked when they are fresh; or the beans may be dried and later soaked for winter use. There are no distinctive divisions, however, as many varieties can be used in more than one way, especially when grown in the garden where commercial pressures do not apply.

It is mostly for a fresh green vegetable that French beans have been – and still are – grown in the UK. They were introduced from America sometime after the 1500s: John Parkinson mentions them in the early 1600s but '...more oftentimes at rich men's tables than at the poor'. Their popularity had increased by the Victorian era, but they were usually just plainly boiled as an accompaniment to meat dishes, and compared with other crops there were relatively few varieties in the seed catalogues. Some had been selected for early forcing, so that Victorian kitchen gardeners could produce out-of-season crops. 'We by no means make such good use of the kidney bean in its many and valuable dried forms as the French.' said William Robinson in 1885. Nor did the range of varieties that we grew compare with that across the Atlantic, where they have been cultivated for many thousands of years, and most of the many beans coming into the American seed trade during the 19th century were local types grown by the Indians.

Modern varieties of French beans in present UK catalogues are nearly all intended for use as green beans. Recent breeding work has tended to concentrate on producing dwarf types with very fine stringless pods which can be processed whole. In comparison much less attention has been given to climbing beans, although for gardeners these have several advantages: they generally give higher yields in a small space, and traditional varieties of climbing beans are renowned for having a much better flavour than their dwarf counterparts. There are few French bean varieties in mainstream catalogues that are specifically intended for fresh shell beans or for drying. These are not considered worthwhile commercial crops in the UK – partly because of the climate and partly because, except for those that come in tins with tomato sauce, they are not popularly eaten.

Amongst heritage varieties and home-saved strains, however, there is an incredible choice of tasty green beans, as well as of varieties suited for eating as fresh shell beans and for drying. The seeds themselves could make a kaleidoscope, and there are stories behind them that are equally colourful, whether it be from family histories, Victorian seedsmen, or American Indians. Varieties with purple flowers or carmine striped pods are attractive enough for flower borders.

Saving seed

Luckily French beans are very easy to save for seed, and they are one of the most popular crops for home seedsavers. The flowers nearly always self-pollinate, so you only need to take minimal precautions to prevent crossing. Even if different varieties are grown side by side there is usually no problem, but if possible separate them by a few metres or by a row or block of another crop. Even some commercial seed growers may sometimes only separate varieties by as little as 3m.

Growing and roguing

Normally gardeners grow plants for seed saving just as they would an edible crop. In areas with a short growing season, start the seeds off as early as possible to give plenty of time for the pods to mature and dry. Seeds can be pregerminated and/or started off in pots or modules inside (see p33). If you have space, you can grow them on to harvest in a greenhouse or polytunnel – unlike runner beans, they do not need insects for pollination and there is no problem with pod set. Climbing varieties need strong supports such as a wigam of canes, just like runner beans.

Because French beans are such inbreeders, seed can successfully be saved from only a few plants (see p42). However, it is best to grow as many as you can to allow for roguing and selection. As the plants grow it is particularly important to remove any plants with unhealthy looking foliage. Dark spots surrounded by yellowish rings are a sign of halo blight, and patchy yellow mottling is a sign of mosaic virus, both of which are common seed-borne diseases. Some French bean varieties are more susceptible to virus diseases than others. Also look out for any plants that have a different habit from the rest – dwarf ones that start to straggle, for example – or odd ones that have flowers or pods that are not true to type. These plants should not cross pollinate with the others, so you can leave them for picking to eat, but make sure you do not save their seed.

Collecting and cleaning seed

The pods change colour as the seeds mature, the colour depending on the variety, and when they have become dry and parchment-like, they are ready for harvest. Individual ripe pods can be picked off or, with bush varieties, whole plants can be pulled up at this stage if necessary. Bring them in to a warm airy place to let the rest of the seed finish ripening. The seed of climbing varieties ripens over a longer period, and you will usually have to pick off mature pods over a period of several weeks. When the pods have become dry and brittle, the seed can be shelled out by hand and further dried for storage (see p44). Remove any seeds that are blemished, or shrivelled.

Varieties

A few old varieties of French bean are still available from some catalogues, for example: the haricot variety **Comtesse de Chambord**; the 19th century French variety **Mont d'Or**, with pale yellow waxy pods; and the green-podded **Canadian Wonder**, which frequently appears in Victorian gardening books and seed lists '...a robust grower, a good cropper' said William Robinson in the 1880s. Other old commercial varieties are in the Heritage Seed Library, along with local varieties and family heirlooms. Gardeners have often hung on to varieties with coloured pods or unusual seeds which have been difficult to obtain in the past. Although several varieties of purple-podded beans are available commercially, for example, home-saved strains are commonly kept; one in the Heritage Seed Library is an heirloom going back three generations. Strains of pea bean have similarly often survived (see below). American heritage varieties, with their great diversity, are also popular with home seedsavers.

Dwarf

Brighstone bean
A local variety grown by gardeners on the Isle of Wight for many years. The original seed is said to have been washed ashore with a shipwreck in the late 1800s (see p25). The plants are vigorous growers with lilac flowers, and produce straight flat pods, green with dark purple streaks. Seed donor Mr Arnold uses them as fresh green beans (the pods go plain green when cooked), but picks them young before they develop strings. Seeds are elongated kidney-shaped, buff streaked with black. Mrs Gill Quirk from Ryde, who grew the variety on for the Seed Search project, found them '... a trouble free plant to grow', doing well despite the frequently wet and windy summer weather.

Brighstone bean and seed

Scott's bean

A white-seeded bean which makes an excellent haricot. The seeds were first given to Mr De'Ath from Colchester in Essex by a neighbour in 1946, and he has been growing it and saving the dried beans – both for eating and sowing – ever since. It has long (around 20cm) flat medium-green pods and very large, distinctly kidney shaped beans: 'There is no commercial variety like it 'says Mr De'Ath'. The pods are slightly stringy, but make good green beans if picked young; '...fresh beans succulent and tasty, lightly boiled for approx. 6 min' recommend Mr and Mrs Ackland from Cornwall who grew on the bean for the Seed Search project.

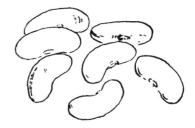

Scott's bean

Brown Soldier

Early Warwick

An old commercial variety grown in England before 1890 and highly commended at the time as one of the earliest green beans. Mr and Mrs Oakley, Heritage Seed Library Guardians for the bean, agree 'This is the earliest producing French bean we have ever grown' they say. The flowers are very pale pink and the pods short, flat and medium green. The pods are tender if picked young, but otherwise can become stringy. The seeds have an attractive colouring – buff streaked with deep maroon – and in late 19th century America were used as an early fresh shelled bean. The Oakleys also use them as a dried bean, as they '...cook well and become creamy in texture'.

Brown Soldier

This bean derives its name from the brownish red markings on the seeds, which resemble a soldier standing to attention. It makes the job of shelling seeds fascinating, and Seed Guardian Mrs Ivy Kelly from Hampshire has even selected the best marked beans from each harvest in order to improve on the soldierly form. The publication *Beans of New York* published in 1931 says Soldier beans were grown in Maine and New Hampshire, and describes them as 'good beans for baking'. However, in its 20 or more years in the Heritage Seed Library members have also found the variety good for eating as young green beans.

Climbing varieties

Ryders Top o' the Pole

When the seed firm Ryders of St Albans went out of business in the early 1970s, Joan Cullen of Eastbourne in Sussex kept this variety going. She also kept some catalogues '...probably out of sentiment' she says. 'I think even my grandparents bought Ryders seeds'. The 1969 issue describes Top o' the Pole as a 'Heavy bearer, absolutely stringless, and of delicious flavour'. The pods are straight, smooth and rounded, and usually at least 20cm long at the ready-to-eat stage. The variety has white flowers and white seeds, which are elongated oval and fairly large – they might make good haricots. 'Of all the beans I have grown, they cropped well above average and are of excellent flavour – completely stringless' said Richard Goulding who grew the variety on for the Seed Search project.

Dinah's Climbing Blue

This purple-podded bean was given to Dinah Butler by her boss at Eynsham, Oxon, in 1971 – she thinks it may have come from France. Dinah has since saved the seed and taken the variety with her to three different gardens. It has dark purplish-green leaves and attractive purple flowers. The pods, which turn green on cooking, are noticeably lacking in strings and parchment compared to some other purple-podded varieties.

Pea bean

This was once a term given to a type of bean with rounded white seeds used for drying, but is now generally used as the name of a variety with maroon/white bicoloured seeds. They are actually commercially available from a few catalogues, but many gardeners have saved their own seed for years – one strain sent to the Seed Search goes back several generations and another to the 1940's Dig for Victory campaign. You cannot help but covet the seeds 'They look like round white peas which have been half-dipped in burgundy ink, complete with the odd spot or two' says Seed Guardian Jennifer Creech. Heritage Seed Library members that grow them generally agree that the plants are resilient, hardy and disease free. They have creamy white flowers and short (10-12cm) pods. These are flat at first, but soon bulge with the shapes of the seeds within. Many gardeners just use pea beans as green beans – the pods are stringless and very tender – but the variety is also ideal for fresh shelled beans ' ...just like fresh peas and broad beans in one, delicious' said Mrs Hemington from Leicestershire who grew one of the strains sent to the Seed Search.

Pea bean

Caseknife

One of the oldest known varieties in America, and listed under this name in seed catalogues here in the mid 1800s although it is probable that this type of bean was grown much earlier. It is a strong climber, and good producer of flat pale green pods shaped like a knife blade. Some Heritage Seed Library members use it as a green bean which, says seed Guardian Mrs J. S. Wilson, it gives in 'quality and quantity', but in America and France it was recommended as a haricot: '... the seed or bean when used fresh from the pod is one of the best' said Vilmorin in 1885.

Bridgwater bean

A family heirloom variety with purple-splashed green pods and large swollen seeds. It was sent to the Seed Search project by Mr Durman of Minehead in Somerset, who had been given some by his cousin Alan Waterjohn from South Petherton near Bridgwater. 'The family have grown the bean for over 50 years' wrote Mr Durman. Alan remembers that 25 or 30 years ago his father-in-law, who had a large garden, used to take some of the beans to the local market: 'people couldn't get enough of them – they had never seen anything like them before' he says. They were apparently always used as green beans, although beans with round, buff and red seeds such as these are similar to those termed 'horticultural beans', which were used mainly freshly shelled or dried.

*Philip Rainford, Seed Guardian for the old commercial
variety of cauliflower St. George.*

Leafy brassicas

(broccoli, Brussels sprouts, cabbage, cauliflower, kale, kohl rabi)

Species: *Brassica oleracea*
Family: *CRUCIFERAE*

Although they look very different to one another when harvested to eat, the vegetables broccoli, Brussels sprouts, cabbage, cauliflower, kale, and kohl rabi are very closely related. They are all modifications of the loose-leaved kale-like plant, similar to the native wild cabbage, that was eaten in very early times: the modern cabbage has been selected for its tight terminal bud, broccoli and cauliflower for their flower tissue, the Brussels sprout for its side buds, and kohl robi for its swollen stem. The link becomes more obvious when the plants are allowed to flower and go to seed – then it is often difficult to tell the different types apart. They are all subspecies of *Brassica oleracea*, with the exception of a few of the kales which belong to *B. napus*. Chinese cabbages and mustards are a different species (*B. campestris = rapa*).

It is not always clear where the brassica entries in early gardening texts fit into the tight modern classification of the crop, but there were many cultivated types even in medieval times. The variations became increasingly sophisticated over the following centuries. William Lucas's seed list in the 1670s, contained over half a dozen different varieties of cabbages, savoys and 'coleworts', and by the mid 1700s, cauliflower, white and purple broccoli, 'turnip cabbage' (kohl rabi) and 'borecoles' (kales) were included in the literature. Then, as now, seed companies were charging much more for new, improved varieties. In 1729, for example, Telfords of York supplied 'best colliflowr.' at a price of 4s (20p) an ounce compared with 6d (2^{1}/$_{2}$p) an ounce for savoy cabbage. Brussels sprouts were relative latecomers to the scene, probably not appearing in English gardens until around 1800 and not becoming popular until several decades later. In 1852, Suttons still lists merely 'Brussels sprouts – fresh imported seed' with no named varieties.

In Victorian times cabbages were one of the most important market garden crops. However, they tended to be largely ignored by the gentry except for the early spring cabbages and red cabbages. The latter were used for pickling and as a traditional accompaniment for roast partridge. In the kitchen gardens of the large country houses, it was cauliflowers and the various forms of broccoli that the gardeners struggled to produce in continual supply. For more ordinary folk kales were an important standby, being less fussy about growing conditions and able to withstand the winter: '...certainly one of the most generally cultivated winter greens, in country places, that we possess: this may be called the poor man's green.' said an article in the *Cottage Gardener and Country Gentleman* in 1858.

The readiness with which brassicas cross-pollinate and change their characteristics means that varieties are easily lost, and in the past seed did not always live up to its advertised description: '...a parcel of the greatest rubbish that ever a man put in his garden' said a correspondent to the same magazine about a packet of so-called Cottagers kale he had received! However, this variability does also seem to have encouraged growers to save their own seed in order to get good strains. In 1885 William Robinson describes how, for this reason, market gardeners around London saved their own cabbage seed, and it certainly led to the emergence of many different local varieties. Right up until the 1960s, for example, even neighbouring villages in the Vale of Evesham had their own strains of Brussels sprouts – varieties such as Evesham Special, Evesham Blue, the Bretforton and Rous Lench, all of which had their own distinctive characteristics.

With the introduction of F1 hybrids, most of these soon disappeared – and much of the genetic variation of the crop along with them. F1 hybrid cabbages and Brussels sprouts, developed to give uniform size, shape and harvest time for commercial growers, started appearing in garden seed catalogues in the late 1960s and early 1970s, and now predominate. In their 2000 catalogue, for example, Thompson & Morgan listed 16 cabbages, 15 of which were F1 hybrids. Calabrese and cauliflowers soon followed – 75% of the cauliflowers grown commercially are now F1s – and more recently the first F1 varieties of kale and purple sprouting broccoli have become widely available. Some breeding programmes are now looking at the resistance of brassicas to a range of pests and diseases, such as cabbage root fly and clubroot.

Saving seed

Brassicas have a reputation of being difficult to save for seed. The main problem is keeping varieties true to type, but in addition, nearly all of them are large and are biennial, taking up space for a relatively long time. The plants are also prey to more than their fair share of pests and diseases. However, don't be discouraged: in the right situation, saving seed from hardy overwintering brassicas such as kale and spring cabbage can be very simple, and the plants produce large amounts of easy-to-collect seed which will keep for four or five years. It doesn't necessarily mean sacrificing an edible harvest either.

Numbers of plants

The more plants you can grow the better. First, this will allow plenty of leeway for loss through pests and disease, and for roguing and selection (see later). Second, all brassicas are primarily outbreeders and are mostly 'self-incompatible' – that is, any individual plant is unable to fertilise itself (see p35). (There are just a few exceptions e.g. summer cauliflower where self-pollination can occur.) Therefore, the more plants that you allow to flower and seed, the better the pollination and subsequent seed production will usually be – and the less likely it is that the variety will suffer from inbreeding depression (see p42). Plant breeders and seed companies maintaining a variety would normally save seed from at least 20-30 plants, but in a garden, there is rarely space for that many. A minimum of six may give satisfactory results in some cases, but grow more if you can.

Growing and roguing

Grow the plants in a seedbed or in modules, and plant them out just as you would a crop grown to eat. If you are growing a known variety, make sure you sow it at the correct time of year for that variety so that you can assess the plants under the right conditions. Cabbages and cauliflowers in particular are usually classified according to the season in which they are ready to harvest. As the plants grow, reject any that are obviously unhealthy or that bolt prematurely. When the plants reach the ready-to-eat stage, it is essential to choose the best, true-to-type plants for seed saving and mark them clearly.

Overwintering

Nearly all leafy brassica crops need a period of winter cold before they will flower and produce seed.

For those normally eaten as winter vegetables – **Brussels sprouts**, **kale**, and **winter cabbage** for example – this is no problem. There can even be some edible harvest without affecting seed production: you can eat some of the leaves from each kale plant, for example, and the lower buttons and top head of brussels sprouts before the leaving the plants to go on to flower. With **winter cabbage**, it can help to cut a cross in the top tightly folded outer leaves to help the flower stalk emerge in early spring. Selected plants of all these crops can usually be moved during the winter without any ill effects – this can save space and allow them to be caged if necessary (see later).

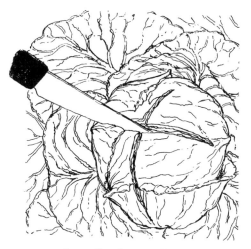

Cut to allow flower stalk to emerge

Spring cabbage and **winter cauliflower** (heading broccoli) are normally overwintered to give a late spring or early summer harvest, so these too will usually flower and produce seed during the summer with few problems. It is quite acceptable to cut the heads of spring cabbage for eating and then let flowering shoots come from the stump. Thinning out the heads of cauliflowers may help to prevent the head rotting as well as giving an edible harvest – leave just a few florets to shoot and produce seed.

Summer and **autumn cabbage** which would normally have been harvested before winter are not so hardy. However, they may stand until spring in mild areas, or if cloched or moved to a polytunnel. Another alternative is to cut off the top two thirds of the head (which would be likely to rot) and leave the stumps to produce flower stalks. **Kohl rabi** may similarly overwinter with protection, but otherwise the swollen 'bulbs' can be lifted and stored in frost free conditions just like carrots or beetroot.

The type of brassica that presents real difficulties for gardeners is the late summer and autumn heading cauliflowers. Their curds readily rot during winter even with protection. Plant breeders and seed companies maintaining varieties in this country use relatively sophisticated methods, sometimes involving taking cuttings or grafting, to overcome this difficulty.

Pollination and isolation

Broccoli, Brussels sprouts, cabbages, cauliflowers and most kales will readily cross-pollinate with each other, the pollen being carried mainly by bees and flies. So for example, not only will a variety of cabbage that you are saving for seed cross with another cabbage, but it will also cross with any sprouting broccoli that is flowering nearby at the same time. These garden crops may also cross with some agricultural brassicas and their escapes in hedgerows and on waste ground. Commercial seed growers are recommended to have up to 1500m between different types of *B.oleracea* (e.g. between cabbage and broccoli) and 1000m between two varieties of the same type (e.g. between two cabbages).

Despite this, in some garden situations where there are no other brassicas growing nearby – or if these are strictly removed at the edible stage – cross-pollination is relatively unlikely. You will be able to let the bees freely enjoy the masses of yellow flowers that your plants produce. However if there are likely to be other brassicas flowering nearby, you will have to physically isolate the plants in a mesh cage and use blowflies to pollinate them. This can be successful, although you can expect a flower set of only about 40% and you will need a relatively tall cage to accommodate the larger brassicas. The seed stalks can reach at least as high again as the original height of the plant, so even short varieties of kales can easily grow to 2m when in flower, for example, and will usually need staking.

Collecting and drying seed

As the seeds ripen, the seed stalk and pods begin to turn brown and dry. At this stage you may need to protect the plants from birds, who will often be just as keen to collect seed as you. The dry pods will also tend to shatter, so you need to make sure that seed is not lost by simply falling to the ground. There are various ways of doing this. One is to collect it as it ripens by going round every few days breaking open the dry pods into a container. More practical for most people is to cut off the individual flower stalks when all the pods are brown and the oldest at the bottom of the stalk are beginning to shatter, then bring them into a warm place to finish drying.

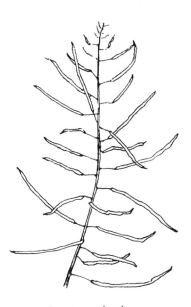

Brassica seed pods

At the Heritage Seed Library, brassica seed stalks are put into paper sacks which are hung in a well-ventilated greenhouse. Mrs Fardell from Cornwall, who grew the summer cabbage Paddy for the Seed Search project, said she spread the drying stalks on a sheet draped over a double bed (presumably in the spare room...). Audrey Adcock has her own method: 'Birds love the seed' she says 'and if any are to be saved, the chosen plants should be swathed in horticultural fleece secured with clothes pegs while the pods are still green. When the pods are brown and dry, tie the stems before cutting and remove the still-wrapped bundle to a dry place. Many pods will have opened, but seeds will be retained by the fleece'.

Pods that have not spontaneously opened and lost their seeds as they dry can be broken open by hand, or by lightly treading on or beating the sack or sheet. The latter may seem harsh, but should not damage the seeds. One account of threshing brassica seeds in the 1930s describes how the seed stalks were laid on a 'stack cloth' pegged out over a layer of straw bedding which acted as cushioning. A man would then walk two horses round and round on top, pressing out the seed (and another man would catch any dung in a bucket as it fell!).

Once the seeds have been removed from the stalks, most of the chaff will be made up of empty pods which can quickly be separated with a course sieve. Any smaller pieces can be removed by winnowing.

Varieties

The number of traditional open-pollinated varieties of each brassica crops still available depends on how widely it is grown as a commercial crop and how much recent attention it has seen from plant breeders. Unfortunately, not many gardeners save brassicas for seed, and local or heirloom varieties are hard to come by. Kales are the exception. In true cottage garden style, gardeners have kept different strains of kale going for years, often using the summer thinnings as 'collards' and the shoots in spring as sprouting broccoli, as well as having a staple winter harvest of leaves. Two strains of kale sent to the Seed Search were family heirlooms going back at least 100 and maybe 150 years.

Sprouting broccoli
Unnamed and relatively 'unimproved' strains of purple sprouting broccoli are still widely available – and up until fairly recently a few market gardeners saved their own seed. Only in the last few years have F1 hybrids been produced. The opposite is the case with green sprouting broccoli, or calabrese, which has a large commercial market. Breeding work on these has concentrated on producing hybrids giving large extremely uniform heads within a very short harvest period. Nevertheless, some catalogues sell open-pollinated 'green sprouting' which would probably suit many gardeners better.

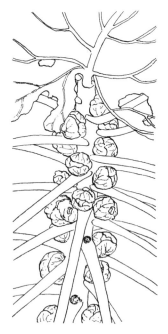

Brussels sprouts
Hardly any gardeners save their own strains, and the majority of varieties in catalogues are F1 hybrids. Nevertheless, a few traditional varieties such as **Seven Hills** and **Evesham Special** are available. The variety **Noisette**, said to be a French heirloom, has long been a favourite at HDRA's Ryton Organic Gardens – it is more compact than many open-pollinated varieties and the sprouts are dense and nutty.

Brussel sprout Noisette

Cauliflowers and heading broccoli (winter cauliflower)

A great many traditional varieties have disappeared and are continuing to do so, although traditional open-pollinated types such as **All Year Round**, useful for spring and autumn sowings, can still be obtained. Hardly any gardeners seem to save their own strains. This can be tricky, but is by no means impossible: Philip Rainford from Preston in Lancashire, for example, is Seed Guardian for the old commercial variety St George. His plants successfully produce impressive 'football-sized' white heads, the first becoming ready for harvest at the end of March from a May sowing. St George was listed in gardening books and seed lists in the 1940s and remained on the National List until the early 1990s.

Kohl rabi

Only recently have substantially 'improved' varieties and F1 hybrids been introduced, generally ousting those such as **White Vienna** and **Purple Vienna** that until recently were the only ones to appear in catalogues. However, these traditional varieties can still be obtained if you look for them. Kohl rabi has always been more popular in Germany and Eastern Europe, where more heritage varieties remain – some reputedly vast in size.

Cabbage

Despite the proliferation of F1 hybrids, there are still some traditional open-pollinated varieties available in mainstream catalogues – particularly of spring cabbages such as **April** (pre 1897), **Offenham** (pre 1897), and **Flower of Spring** (pre 1905). There are also modern selections of old favourites such as the summer cabbage **Golden Acre**, and the winter cabbages **Christmas Drumhead** and **January King**. A few gardeners save their own strains often selected for large heads. For example, seed of the summer/autumn cabbage **Paddy**, sent to the Seed Search by Peter Jones of Camberley, had originally been given to his father around 25 years ago by an Irish allotment holder who had selected the strain for the size of its large flat heads.

Kale

The long cottage garden tradition of kale – and the lack of interest in it as a commercial crop – seems to have helped many old varieties and home-saved strains survive.

Ragged Jack

'Ragged' is an extremely good description of this variety: the glaucous grey-green leaves are deeply divided and crested – Vilmorin describes them as being 'slashed'. The plants are short – often around 50cm high – with a purple tinge in the stems and leaf stalks which tends to extend to the leaves in winter, and can make them stunning to look at. Ragged Jack was widely grown in the early 1800s. It was '...very well known also in the cottage and farm gardens,' say the Transactions of the

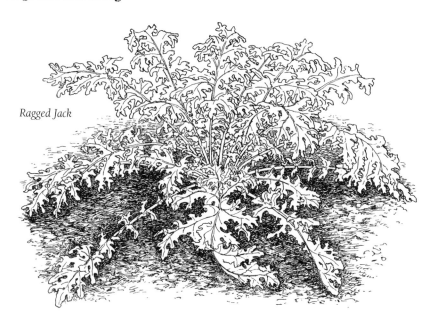

Ragged Jack

Horticultural Society in 1816/17 'but in the seed shops it is a great stranger'. References to it occur in horticultural literature right up until the 1950s, and gardeners have continued to grow it, and keep home-saved strains in cultivation.

Paul Pickering, for example, had a strain that his family had been growing for years as 'Tunley Greens'. It had originally been obtained by his wife's grandfather from Tunley in Wiltshire in 1910. Peter Handy's strain 'Theyer', which he sent to the Seed Search project, can be traced back to his aunt's grandfather John Theyer of Tewkesbury. From the 1890s it was grown by Mr Theyer's two spinster daughters, and then by their two nieces (his aunts), before seed was passed to him in the 1950s. One of the longest histories goes with the Canadian Ragged Jack grown by Mrs Shuker of Bath, which had originally been taken to Canada by an English family somewhere around the middle of the 19th century (see p26).

Ragged Jack is a valuable source of winter greens – the leaves are sweet and tender, despite their apparently tough looks – and it also gives welcome young shoots in spring. Audrey Adcock from Tiverton, who grows a local 'Sidborough' strain says: 'In spring we eat the flower buds picked with stems 4-6 inches long with 2-4 leaves attached. Steam until tender. WE think the flavour is delicious.'

Ragged Jack is sometimes considered a synonym of Red Russian kale – a variety said to have been introduced into Canada and Alaska by Russian traders. Red Russian is certainly very similar in appearance, although is possibly taller with more of a purple tinge than some of the strains of Ragged Jack. Red Russian has recently appeared in mainstream seed catalogues, and somewhat ironically, was awarded an Award of Garden Merit from the RHS in its 1999-2000 kale trials.

Asparagus Kale

In Victorian times, the young shoots of what was called Asparagus Kale were a real spring delicacy. 'Where there is room for a row we would advise all readers to appropriate it to the Asparagus Kale' said the *Journal of Horticulture* in 1871 '... the great attraction is the multitude of shoots it throws out ...and these taken clean off when from 3 inches to 4 inches in length, are in reality a good sweet substitute for the shoots of asparagus.' Although they all agree about the shoots, old descriptions of the actual Asparagus Kale plant vary and possibly more than one type was used in this way.

However, the variety kept by the Heritage Seed Library is certainly of the type recognised as Asparagus Kale in the 1920s and 1930s. 'This seed is a direct line from the Asparagus Kail [sic] which we have been growing since 1937' said Jeremy Inglis from Oban who sent the variety to the Heritage Seed Library in 1986. It has medium green plain leaves on relatively short, compact plants. The young leaves can be eaten over the winter months, and then the young shoots in spring. Seed Guardian Mary Eastwood from Altrincham does not sow it until August, and says it still grows enough before winter to form a good base: '...I now prefer it to traditional purple sprouting broccoli, if it is picked when still young. Very delicious. I use quite a lot of the stem – 6inches [15cm].'

Cottagers Kale

This is a vigorous kale, growing up to 1.5m tall with purple tinged stems and large dark bluish green leaves. It is distinctive for its profusion of rosette-like side shoots, which form in late autumn. 'Picking half a dozen gives you a portion' says Heritage Seed Library member Leslie Hawkins, who uses these small leaves for cooking and in salads, and feeds the large main leaves of the plants to her goats. According to one 19th century garden book, Cottagers Kale was raised at Sherburn Castle in Oxfordshire by crossing one of the varieties there with Brussels sprouts '...it was submitted to the Horticultural Society in the spring of 1858, and is said to be the most tender of all the greens, and of exquisite flavour.' Cottagers Kale remained in cultivation through the 1900s, although in the early 1990s it appeared in only one or two catalogues and looked in danger of being dropped from the National List. However, it survives there today.

Diane Bailey, Seed Guardian for the leek Colossal.

Leek

Species: *Allium porrum*
Family: *ALLIACEAE*

The descriptions of leeks in seed catalogues are rarely inspiring, but in fact there are significant differences between varieties. The most noticeable is the length and girth of the 'shank' or 'shaft', which is the part we eat. This is naturally white to some extent, but the whiteness can be emphasised and extended by deep planting or by blanching it in some other way. The extremes of shape are seen on the show bench, where the straight white shaft of some blanched varieties can reach 40cm or more, compared with the very thick short pot leeks which are measured for the judges in cubic inches.

The 'flag' or leaves of the leek can be militaristically upright or loose and spreading, the latter being useful for organic growers as it can help to suppress weeds. It can vary in colour from pale green to dark blue green, with the variety Bleu de Solaise having purplish tinges which make it popular for its ornamental qualities. The appearance of leek foliage can also be affected by rust, a common disease which appears as powdery orange streaks on the leaves. Some varieties are more susceptible to rust than others. To gardeners who rely on leeks as a late winter staple, hardiness is one of their most important characteristics and is a particular feature of many of the established favourites.

Leeks were grown in Britain in medieval times, and in the 17th century the seedsman William Lucas listed two strains – the London leek and the French leek. A century later, however, little appears to have changed, and even during the Victorian period leeks were only fully appreciated in the north of England and in Scotland.

These areas spawned several popular varieties, such as the Musselburgh leek, still well known today: The crop found little favour with the gentry in the south at the time, and their cooks seemed mostly to have used the vegetable 'well-boiled' or 'well stewed in gravy'. Size was all important, and 'immense', 'very large' and 'splendid specimens' were the sorts of words used to advertise nearly all varieties in the catalogues.

In fact the size of a leek depends on the length of the growing season and on the growing conditions, as well as on variety. The sooner you can start off the seeds and the larger you can get the leek before you transplant it, the better the yield will be. The size of a variety is therefore difficult to assess in a garden if you only grow one or two different ones every year. Despite the traditional quest for large leeks, small ones can be more versatile for the kitchen – steamed whole, or sliced thinly for stir fries, or even raw in salads.

In today's catalogues, leeks are usually classified according to when they mature: from the quick growing early leeks which you can harvest in September to the hardy late types which will stand until May. Early varieties traditionally have longer shafts and lighter green foliage, and late varieties are stockier with darker leaves. However, breeding has tended to increase the length of naturally white shank of both types, and has also aimed to produce varieties with resistance to specific diseases and to bolting. In addition, many modern varieties have erect foliage, which allows them to be grown at closer spacings and makes them easier to pack for the supermarket. An increasing number are F1 hybrids.

Saving seed

Leeks are biennial and also cross-pollinate, but this does not necessarily make them difficult to save for seed. They will usually easily overwinter outside, and if you only grow one variety for seed, foreign pollen from elsewhere is unlikely to be a problem. It is almost worth it just to see the beautiful spherical purple flowerheads, loved by bees. The main problem is getting seed to ripen in wet autumns.

Leeks can also be propagated from 'pips' (bulblets that form in the flowerhead) instead of from seed. However, pips can easily carry over leek rust disease, so for maintaining and passing on a variety, it is preferable to save seed.

Growing and roguing

In the first year, grow the crop just as you would for eating, removing any plants that bolt. In late autumn choose the plants that you are going to use for seed. Leeks are strong outbreeders, and you should ideally keep at least 16, preferably more, in order to maintain the health and genetic diversity of the variety. Exclude any that are weak, or very different from the rest in size, length of shaft, or in the width and colour of the leaf. You can transplant them if necessary at this stage, to space them about 30cm apart in a row or in a block. Many varieties will overwinter in the ground with no problem, but you may need to protect less hardy varieties in severe weather. If you have space, leeks can benefit from being grown in a polytunnel or greenhouse from this stage to seed harvest, as the heads are slow to mature and ripen.

In late spring stout cylindrical flower spikes will start to emerge with the flowerhead enclosed in a papery sheath. These will usually need staking. For Heritage Seed Library Guardian Diane Bailey from Surrey, this is one of the few times the plants grown for seed need special attention: 'I weed them once' she says 'and spend an afternoon attaching the flowerheads to canes to stop the wind breaking them off'.

Pollination and isolation

The many small flowers that make up the leek flowerhead open over an extended period and generally do not self pollinate (they are 'protandrous' – see p36). Pollen is carried by bees and other insects from flower to flower on the same and different plants.

Leeks can cross-pollinate with other leeks that are in flower but not with onions, so only if you are growing more than one variety for seed or there are other flowering leeks in the area, will you need to physically isolate the plants. You can use a mesh cage and introduce blowflies (see p38-40). Commercial seed producers are generally recommended to isolate different leek crops for seed by a minimum distance of 1000m, although distances down to about 300m have been considered satisfactory in the past for standard seed.

Harvesting and cleaning seed

Seeds on individual flowerheads mature over an extended period, becoming black when they are ripe and easily seen against the silvery seed capsules. They ripen late – much later than onions – and will not dry outside if the autumn weather is poor. Before there is any danger of frost, cut the heads with about 20cm of stalk. Spread them out to dry on a sheet, or hang them in paper sacks, in a warm dry airy place until the seeds begin to separate readily from their capsules.

As the heads dry, much of the seed will fall out of the opening seed capsules, and you can help it by shaking the heads or gently rubbing the capsules with your fingertips – the drier they are, the easier it will come out. The harvested seed should therefore be fairly clean and any chaff – which will usually be much lighter – can be removed by winnowing (see p46).

Propagating leeks from pips

These tiny bulblets sometimes grow naturally between the fine flower stalks on the spherical flowerheads of leeks. You can encourage their formation by shaving off the flowerbuds with a razor blade just before they open, leaving the stalks. When the pips ripen, they can be broken off and planted rather like onion sets, although they are much smaller – only about 6mm in length.

Varieties

Several old commercial varieties – or modern selections of them – are still available from some catalogues. These include **Giant Winter** (see below) and the Victorian varieties **Musselburgh** and **The Lyon**. The Musselburgh leek is said to have been raised by James Hardcastle of

Propagating leeks from pips

Musselburgh in the 1830s and The Lyon leek introduced by seedsmen Stuart & Mein from Kelso around 1883. Other old commercial varieties are in the Heritage Seed Library. There seems to be few family heirloom leeks, but many exhibition growers save their own strains for showing – although usually from pips, because this gives them well shaped leeks with shafts that are less likely to bulb at the base than those of leeks grown for seed.

Colossal

A Victorian variety producing short stout leeks. Webb's catalogue for 1888 describes it as 'rapid in growth and extremely hardy'. Heritage Seed Library members find that it rarely matches the 'immense size' it was credited with it in those times, but it is a reliable cropper. Guardian Diane Bailey finds that it is very easy to grow, although can suffer from rust. 'It will stand until required for eating during late autumn and winter – until April or longer' she says.

Early Market

A traditional early leek, not deleted from the National List until the early 1990s. Suttons catalogue described it as 'A very early maturing variety for use in autumn'. Its shaft is straight with minimal bulbing. Heritage Seed Library Guardian Catherine Gandolfi says it has ' a good mild leeky flavour'.

Giant Winter

A late maturing leek, introduced in the early 1900s and still available from some mainstream seed catalogues. It has dark green foliage and a short stem (about 9cm) with some tendency to bulb at the base, but nevertheless gives a good if not massive yield late in the season. In a NIAB (National Institute for Agricultural Botany) trial for organic growers in 1993/4, it showed good resistance to rust, and it has a well-deserved reputation for hardiness. The gardeners at Ryton Organic Gardens remember that it was the only leek variety to survive on the then very exposed site during the harsh winter of 1986/7.

Bleu de Solaise

This is said to be an old French heirloom, listed by some seed companies as synonymous with the variety St Victor Blue. It is a hardy late-maturing variety unique for the purplish tinge on its leaves. This becomes more exaggerated in cold weather and the plants look stunning in winter potagers, as a divider or edging for green leafy crops. The leeks have relatively long stems (about 18cm) and in the NIAB trials (see above) gave yields comparable to many of the modern varieties, although it was found to be susceptible to rust.

Mammoth Pot Leek

Mammoth Pot Leek

The only pot leek to be registered on the National List, this has been grown and saved for seed on the nursery of the family seed company Robinsons & Sons of Lancashire since the late 1800s. The leeks have short white shafts about 13cm long and are very thick – their circumference can reach around 30cm in normal garden conditions. Margaret and Susan who now run the nursery, and whose great grandfather introduced the variety, say that although the pot leek is grown mainly by exhibitors, other gardeners are becoming interested in it. This is partly because it is very hardy, and partly because of its delicate mild flavour.

*Peter Andrews of Bath Organic Group with seed heads
of the Bath Cos lettuce.*

Lettuce

Species: *Lactuca sativa*
Family: *COMPOSITAE*

John Evelyn used the terms 'cabbage' and 'cos' to describe lettuce in his 17th century Salad Calendar, and together with the category of loose-headed 'leaf' or 'cutting' lettuce, this is still the main way of classifying the crop today.

As well as the type of head it forms, the texture, appearance and taste of a lettuce are all equally important. The rounded cabbage lettuces vary from the soft – sometimes sadly limp – leaves of the butterhead lettuces to the wrinkled brittle leaves of the crispheads. Cos lettuce have long crisp upright leaves, but these often form only a fairly loose heart. This is particularly true of older varieties which were sometimes tied up with raffia to blanch the inner leaves. Nevertheless cos lettuces have the best reputation for flavour. Loose leaf lettuces with their colours, curls and frills are the most decorative type, but do not always have the taste to match.

Many lettuces have one specific time of year when they grow best. This depends on the conditions they need to heart, how quickly they bolt, and how hardy they are. It is important to use the right varieties for the right seasons to get the best results.

Surprisingly perhaps for a vegetable that is not a major food crop, lettuces feature strongly in early seed catalogues. Eight types or varieties were listed by seedsman William Lucas in the late 1600s and nearly double this figure appear a century later, the lists including 'red' and 'spotted' lettuces as well as simple cabbage and cos types. Less unexpected is the number in cultivation in Victorian times: one writer estimated that there were 'not less than 50'. Despite this, their use of the crop seems to have been decidedly unimaginative. Giving advice to gardeners in 1885, the seed company

Sutton & Sons suggests keeping to the leading varieties, not 'departing from these types for mere sake of variety or novelty', and red lettuces were talked of as curiosities. According to one traveller, British salads were a 'mass of flabby green' compared to those in France, which were carefully prepared dishes. The French regularly used 'oak-leaved' and curled and crisp 'endive-leaved' cutting lettuces of the sort that rarely appeared in UK catalogues until the 1970s.

Modern breeding has tended to increase the uniformity of varieties and standardise their harvest times. It has also produced varieties for more specific growing conditions and periods of use – in particular ones suited to winter production under glass, which for commercial growers have replaced the coarser (but possibly more tasty) hardy types. If you want a winter lettuce to grow out in the garden, it is certainly worth trying some of the old types. Modern varieties are also often bred to be resistant to diseases such as botrytis or downy mildew but some older ones have shown themselves to have good resistance too.

Saving seed

Provided the weather conditions are good, lettuce can be an easy crop to save for seed. It is an annual and is largely self-pollinating.

Growing and roguing

One of the main problems is the length of time it takes for seedheads to form and the seeds to ripen, particularly with dense crisphead varieties. A few days of wet autumn weather can easily cause the seedheads to go mouldy. Kathy Kromm from Cheltenham who has been Heritage Seed Library Guardian for the lettuce Stoke for the last ten years says 'The weather plays a major part in getting a long enough growing season to get seed'. Whilst she has found it very easy during hot summers such as 1995, in poor summers little or no seed could be harvested.

Lettuce seedhead

You can help get around the problem in several ways. Sow hardy winter lettuce in early autumn and overwinter the plants in a greenhouse or cold frame, or under cloches, the advantage of this being that they should then flower and seed early the following summer. Summer lettuce should be started off as early in spring as possible, either sowing direct or preferably in blocks or modules in a greenhouse. If you have space, grow them on for seed in the greenhouse or in a polytunnel, avoiding problems with wet weather. As an alternative Kathy Kromm tried growing them in large pots on a patio, so she could move them around to get more sun or shelter.

Whether you are growing plants outside or in a greenhouse border, space them about 45cm in a row or in a block – giving them plenty of space helps avoid problems with botrytis, and helps the seedheads to dry. As lettuce are strong inbreeders, you can successfully maintain a variety by saving seed from just one or two plants (see p42), but aim for more than this if possible. Starting with about 10 plants should allow for roguing, and rotting off or other mishaps which may prevent plants reaching the seeding stage. You should get more than enough seed even from a few plants: one wartime gardening book estimates that a well-grown lettuce plant will yield as many as 30,000 seeds 'an ample sufficiency to offset the occasional disastrous summer', and Heritage Seed Library Guardians have obtained an average of up to 15g of seed per plant – although this does depend on growing conditions and on variety.

As the plants grow, water them regularly in dry spells. Remove any that are very different to the rest in leaf shape or colour, or in the formation of the head. If any plants are stunted and/or have leaves that show pale green mottling or are abnormally crinkled, remove them immediately as these are symptoms of lettuce mosaic virus which is a common seed-borne disease. Also pull up any plants which bolt much earlier than the rest, as saving seed from these will increase the variety's tendency to bolt in future generations.

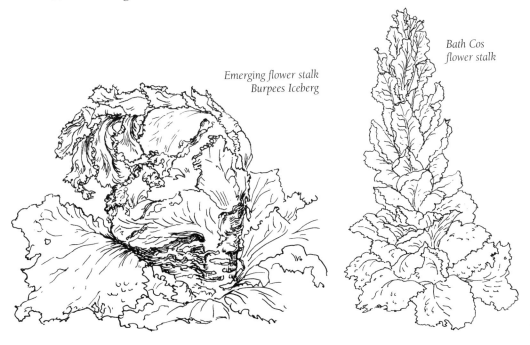

*Emerging flower stalk
Burpees Iceberg*

*Bath Cos
flower stalk*

Once the lettuces have passed the pick-to-eat stage, flower stalks will start to form. In some varieties that form a very firm head, the stalk may have difficulty in pushing its way out and you will need to help it. Gently peel the leaves away just enough to expose the stalk as it emerges. The closely packed leaves of these varieties also makes them more prone to botrytis, particularly in wet weather, so carefully remove any dead or rotting foliage from around the stem, taking care not to break off any flower shoots. The flower stalks may need staking as they grow taller.

Pollination and isolation

Although the tiny individual lettuce flowers are generally self-pollinating, a small amount of cross-pollination is said to occur in some cases. If you are growing more than one variety for seed, take the precaution of separating each by two or three metres or by another tall crop. Cultivated lettuce can also cross with the wild lettuce *Lactuca serriola* ('prickly lettuce'), but this is not usually a garden weed and only commonly found on waste ground in the south east of England.

Harvesting and cleaning seed

The seeds on each plant ripen gradually over a period of a few weeks, forming white plumes like thistle seeds. Ideally seed should be collected every two or three days from the growing plants during that period, by shaking it into a paper sack. However, in short growing seasons and wet conditions, it is often better to pull up whole plants. Wait until you can see the white fluff of the seeds on about 50% of the flowerheads of a particular plant, then lift it gently and hang it upside down inside large paper sack in a warm, dry, airy place to allow the seeds to carry on ripening.

When the stems of the hanging plants are brittle to the touch and the seeds have all produced fluff, they will be ready for cleaning. As long as the seed capsules are really dry and open, the seeds with their plumes should be released easily. If necessary, the plumes and any remaining bits of seed capsule can be separated by rubbing the seeds gently on a sieve to abrade them away. This will also help to remove some of the larger debris. The smaller pieces can be removed by winnowing (see p46), although this needs great care as seeds are relatively light. The favourite method of Katie Butler, Head Gardener at Yalding Organic Gardens, is to shake the seeds and chaff gently on a sheet of newspaper – the fluffy bits of seedhead should gradually come to the surface and drift off the paper or can be easily removed.

Varieties

Around half a dozen Victorian varieties – or modern selections of them – still survive in today's catalogues. These include some familiar names such as the quick-growing dwarf variety **Tom Thumb** and the butterhead **All The Year Round**; also the red curly leaved French heirloom **Marvel of the Four Seasons**; and the original iceberg **Batavia Blonde** (see overleaf). A number of gardeners save their own lettuce seeds, and there are several handed-down varieties in the Heritage Seed Library. Traditional leaf lettuces from abroad, such as the French **Feuille de Chene** (oak leaf), have long been popular with home seedsavers – since well before similar varieties began to appear in mainstream catalogues.

Bath Cos

This variety appears in some seed lists of the late 18th and early 19th century and it remained popular throughout Victorian times, being especially recommended as an autumn and winter lettuce. Good crops can be obtained from August sowings. The variety was also sometimes grown in summer and some Heritage Seed Library members successfully use it this way, although 'it can bolt at the drop of a seed packet' says Peter Andrews from the Bath Seed Saving Group. It is a large lettuce, with long (30-40cm) robust leaves: the outer ones dull, but the inner ones a fresh lime green. They form a loose head which in the past was usually tied up to make it a contrasting white inside, although this is not essential. Despite its rather coarse appearance when growing, Bath cos really does have superb flavour, and who could resist the description of it given by a contributor to *The Gardener* in 1867: 'Thrown into a heap on the snowy linen, it looks a rich crystalline, frothy pile and cannot fail to be a tempting and refreshing bite for the hungry sportsman after a hard days labour.' The variety is brown seeded.

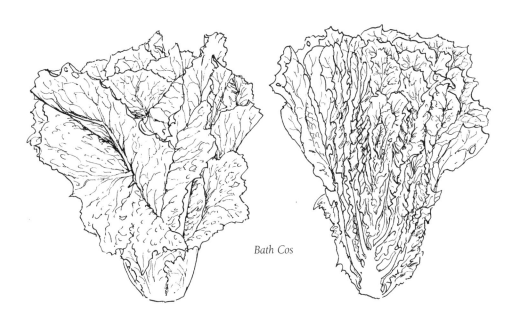

Bath Cos

Iceberg or Batavia Blonde

Although the term 'iceberg' has now been adopted for the type of large solid white lettuces found prepacked in supermarkets, it is in fact the name of a specific old variety. It is a crisphead with light green outer leaves and a crunchy but less dense heart than the modern types. It has been grown since the 1850s, but is still listed in the EC common catalogue, and illustrates just how important old varieties can turn out to be. Iceberg was found to have unique type of resistance to downy mildew, being less susceptible to all races of the disease – so much so that in the 1990s the variety was used in a plant breeding programme at HRI Wellesbourne aimed at breeding disease resistance into modern crisphead lettuce varieties. Iceberg is white seeded.

Loos Tennis Ball

'Tennis ball' is a general name given to quite a few old lettuces, presumably referring to their rounded shape, and there are references to several varieties in horticultural literature in the late 18th and the 19th century. Loos Tennis Ball was offered by several seed companies in the 1930s as a good lettuce for indoor use. It is a butterhead variety, forming a large, loose, more or less spherical head of light green leaves. Heritage Seed Library Guardian Jim Plummer recalls how the lettuce was grown on his father's commercial nursery at Warton in Lancashire in the 1930s and 1940s. It was sown both for a 'backend' maturing crop and as spring-maturing variety under glass. 'He found Loos Tennis Ball to be the best of those he tried' says Mr Plummer 'It was an appealing light green and so showed up well when displayed on the market wholesalers' stalls in Manchester and other towns; but above all, it was 99.5% immune to mildew. This was vital, especially in those days, long before the advent of increased artificial light in greenhouses.' Loos Tennis Ball is white-seeded.

Soulie

A French heirloom lettuce grown by the Soulie family from Vabre in Tarn. Luc Soulie, now in his sixties, saves the seed every year as his father did before him, and no one in the area can put a name to the lettuce. In the 1990s Luc gave some seed to some English friends who started growing the variety at home in Glasgow, and subsequently sent it to the Seed Search project. It is a medium-sized cos lettuce with relatively soft long leaves which are green with a bronze tint, particularly under stress. They form a fairly loose heart. Soulie grew well as a summer lettuce at the Heritage Seed Library in 2000 and gained unanimous approval for flavour: 'Neither bland nor bitter, but a real taste to it' said the Senior Horticulturalist Neil Munro.

Stoke

A small hardy cos type lettuce with slightly pointed dark green leaves. 'The leaves are meaty and wrinkled, like Little Gem' says Guardian Kathy Kromm, who finds that they taste 'just fine', even when the plants are beginning to bolt. The original seed came to the Heritage Seed Library at least 20 years ago from Stoke near Rochester in Kent, where it had been grown for 150 years by the Cheeseman family. Probably, it was said, the variety originated years before that – to a time when winter lettuces were grown outdoors, rather than being grown under glass or imported from Spain. HSL members in the south of England have certainly overwintered it outside with no protection. The variety is black seeded.

Bronze Arrow

A non-hearting leaf lettuce, said to be an heirloom from California but popular with Heritage Seed Library members here. The plants are large and the leaves, which are pointed like an arrowhead, have a distinct bronze tint. 'Lovely to look at, would grace a flower border' said Guardian A. Kennedy. Hardy and slow to bolt. Good for summer and autumn sowings.

Melon

Species. *Cucumis melo*
Family: *CUCURBITACEAE*

The fruits of melons can vary enormously both in their size and external appearance, and in the colour of the flesh inside – as well of course as in flavour. The smooth yellow-skinned types with watery green flesh that come from Africa to the supermarkets are quite different from those that can be grown in a greenhouse at home, and different again from the oriental types which look, and are used, more like cucumbers or squashes. Classifications are abundant but confusing, as melons readily cross pollinate and there are many intermediate types. To gardeners it is a meltingly sweet flesh and the ability to ripen in our short cool summers which are the important qualities to combine.

It is unlikely that the melons that appeared in early English seed lists tasted like this. They were apparently treated more like a vegetable, flavoured with vinegar, salt, and pepper, or perhaps even cooked to prepare them for the table. By the late 18th century hardy rough-skinned 'canteloups' were being grown, but it was the Victorians with their hot beds and heated glasshouses who developed melons as among the 'very choicest dessert fruit'. Whilst the cantaloupes occupied frames, finely netted 'musk' melons hung in nets in special melon houses piped with hot water, and it was these varieties that were most prized for flavour.

Many head gardeners on the large country estates saved seed of melons and developed their own strains, just as they did with cucumbers and onions. Both prestige and profit were to be gained from those varieties which won awards at the shows, as the tale of Thomas Crump and his Blenheim Orange melon illustrates (see Varieties).

What a scandal, therefore, when according to the *Journal of Horticulture* in 1868, a show judge pilfered some seeds from inside one of the exhibited fruit!

Almost none of the robust cantaloupes or tender netted melons from this time are readily availalble today. F1 hybrids, many bred for the North American market, dominate most of the catalogues. The main aims of plant breeders have been to produce varieties with resistance to specific diseases (particularly to powdery mildew, fusarium wilt and some virus diseases); also to produce hardier varieties, standardise harvest times and improve the keeping qualities of the fruit. Some of these qualities are useful for gardeners, but it is doubtful whether the Victorians would approve – for flavour the old types are still worth trying.

Saving seed

Melons can be quite tricky to grow, but collecting the seed is easy (you are almost there when you prepare the fruit to eat) and the crop is quite popular with home seedsavers. Melons will easily cross with other melon varieties, but not with watermelons which are a separate species (*Citrullus lanatus*), or with cucumbers or squashes.

Growing and roguing

Grow the plants exactly as you would for eating: they need starting off in heat and most varieties grow best in a greenhouse or polytunnel. Although melons are outbreeders, you can successfully save seed from just one or two plants if necessary, although it is preferable to have about six.

As the plants grow, remove any that are stunted or that have leaves which are crinkled or mottled, as these could have seed-borne virus diseases.

Pollination and isolation

Like other cucurbits, melons have separate male and female flowers on the same plant. They are usually pollinated by bees or other insects, moving between flowers both on the same and on different plants. It is easiest to grow just one variety both for eating and for seed and let the insects do the pollinating, although it may help to try transferring the pollen yourself as well, using a soft brush. Your neighbours are probably less likely to be growing melons than many other crops, but it is worth checking. If you grow more than one variety yourself or if there are others growing nearby, then you will have to bag and hand pollinate the flowers (see p41), although some seedsavers find that this can be more difficult to do successfully than with cucumbers or squashes. Commercial seed growers are recommended to isolate melon varieties by 500-1000m.

Harvesting and cleaning seed

Luckily seeds of melons are mature just when the fruits are ready to eat, so you can collect seed when you pick for the table. Select fruits of typical size, and which have a skin and flesh colour which is true to type. When you cut the fruits open, also check that the depth of flesh in comparison to the size of the seed cavity is typical of the variety.

Scrape out the seeds into a bowl and add water. Stir the contents to detach the seeds from any surrounding fibre, then allow to settle and pour off the water and debris. Repeat this process until the seeds are clean, then drain through a sieve and spread them out to dry on a tray or plate – anything that has a shiny surface so that they do not stick. Keep this in a warm airy place and stir the seeds around occasionally to break up any clumps and help them to dry evenly. They are ready for storage when they snap in half, rather than bending.

Varieties

The only Victorian melon still readily available is **Blenheim Orange** (see below). A few other heritage varieties – mainly from the USA or from France – can be found in specialist catalogues or heritage collections, and are popular with home seedsavers.

Hero of Lockinge

In 1881 this variety was heralded by Sutton & Son as 'magnificent', and by Carters as the 'finest new melon of the season'. It has smooth-skinned round fruit, which are light green when immature and ripen to yellow with a slight green mottling. The flesh

Jenny Lind

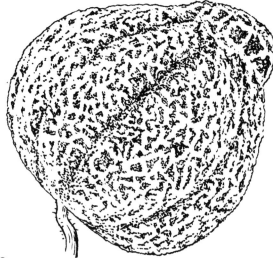

is a delicate pale yellow. It is a variety that would have produced large fruits in the heated melon houses in Victorian times. However, it would be worth trying in an unheated greenhouse in the south of England – gardeners at Yalding Organic Gardens in Kent have successfully produced fair-sized fruit for the Heritage Seed Library in such conditions. However, you should not expect it to ripen until September. Hero of Lockinge remained on the National List right up until 1995, when it disappeared from the seed catalogues.

Blenheim Orange

One of the very few Victorian melons to remain popular, this still survives on the National List. As the name suggests, it was raised at Blenheim by Mr Thomas Crump, Head Gardener to the Duke of Marlborough. The variety was awarded first prize in the summer show of the Royal Horticultural Society in July 1880, judged the best amongst 30 other melons, and subsequently Mr Crump sold the seed to Mr James Carter's seed company at a cost of 1s 6d per 100. Blenheim Orange produces round netted fruit, dark green with paler stripes when immature but ripening to orange, and has red flesh. Like Hero of Lockinge, it is late to ripen and would do best with some heat, although gardeners at HDRA's Audley End Kitchen Garden have successfully produced fruit without heat in the old peach house there: 'They were small but absolutely delicious' said Head Gardener Mike Thurlow.

Jenny Lind

A heritage variety from the USA, once sold in the UK by Thompson & Morgan, but since dropped from its catalogue and maintained in the Heritage Seed Library. It was named after an opera singer who in mid 19th century America was billed as 'the Swedish nightingale': the fruit's green flesh was said to be as sweet and scented as her voice. In the later part of that century it was grown exclusively for the Philadelphia and New York markets. It is a small, ribbed melon, shaped like a flattened globe with a distinctive knob at the blossom end. The immature fruits are green and strongly netted, ripening to a marbled orangy brown. The variety is relatively hardy and should produce fruit by mid August in an unheated greenhouse in the south of England.

Seed Guardian, Eddie Lancaster hanging up seed heads of the onion Up-to-Date in a greenhouse, to dry.

Onion

Species: *Allium cepa*
Family: *ALLIACEAE*

Brown-skinned, globe-shaped onions now dominate both the supermarket shelves and the seed catalogues, but bulbs in other colours and shapes are still to be had if you look for them. There are those with deep red skins like Red Brunswick, or with papery white ones like Paris Silverskin; there are flattened ones like Brown Spanish and torpedo-shaped ones like Long Red Florence. The flesh of most types is usually white, but the pigment of red-skinned varieties can extend inside the bulb to give rings of white and pink.

Although colour and shape are the most noticeable characteristics of onion bulbs, it is their size and pungency which have most influence on how you use them. Both these factors are affected by growing conditions, but also depend on variety. The large varieties grown for exhibition have the mildest flavour – good for stuffing or for frying in rings. Many of these have the old variety Ailsa Craig in their ancestry. Small strong onions are good for pickling or putting whole in stews. Gardeners wanting continuous supplies of onions also need ones that keep well throughout the winter, and although it does not always say so on the seed packets, some varieties store much better than others.

Different types of onion, varying in colour and shape, were available from the earliest seedsmen: for example, Spanish, Strasbourg, Blood Red, and Silverskin onions were all listed by Stephen Garraway, a merchant in Fleet street in the late 1770s. In Victorian times they remained a popular crop, despite the concerns of the gentry of the day with their unsociable side effects. Both market gardeners and the gardeners of the big country estates had to make them available all year round, and used storage methods very similar to those used by gardeners today. In 1885 William Robinson writes of 'Great breadths of onions .. grown at Fulham, Chiswick, Deptford and Mitcham' and describes how the bulbs that are firm and sound are '...tied into bunches and strung in pairs over poles or pegs in a loft or shed, so that they can be marketed at any convenient season during winter and spring'. Some of the varieties used at the time such as Bedfordshire Champion and James Long Keeping certainly have a reputation for storing well. Victorian gardeners also used hardy varieties of onion for sowing in autumn and overwintering. Given this head start, they would put on rapid growth in spring, and 'washed, which makes them look white' would give a summer harvest of large fresh onions.

Onion flowerheads

Most modern onion varieties are F1 hybrids, bred to give higher yields and to be more uniform in size, shape, colour and harvest time for commercial growers. They come and go rapidly from the catalogues and are often difficult for gardeners to tell apart. The new autumn sown types introduced in the last 20-30 years are different to traditional overwintering types: they not only grow on quickly in spring, but start to bulb and mature earlier, without waiting for the long summer days. They can thus produce a dried onion bulb in summer, which can be marketed in the same way as maincrop onions.

Saving seed

Onions are a biennial crop, and the bulbs must generally be lifted and stored overwinter before seed can be collected the following summer. They also cross pollinate, both with other onion varieties and with multiplier onions such as shallots. However, cross pollination is not always a problem, and the statuesque flower stalks that the bulbs produce can more than compensate for the trouble of storing them.

Growing and roguing

In the first year, grow the crop just as you would for eating. Remove any plants whose leaves look unhealthy or very different in colour or habit from the rest, and any that bolt prematurely. In late summer lift and dry the bulbs as normal, and sort them carefully. As onions are strong outbreeders, ideally you need to grow on at least 16 for seed in order to maintain the health and diversity of the variety (see p42). Discard any that are misshapen, split or have abnormally thick necks, and ones that are diseased, and choose only those of colour, shape and size typical of the variety for seed saving. Store these in a net or tray in a cool, dry, airy frost free place, just as you would your winter supplies for the kitchen. Label them clearly!

The following spring, check that the bulbs are still healthy, and around the time that you would normally plant out your onion sets, replant the good ones. Space them about 30cm in rows or blocks. They should soon sprout furiously and produce tall hollow flowerstalks. As these grow taller and the flowers develop, they will usually need staking.

Isolation and pollination

Like those of leeks, the spherical onion flowerheads are made up of many small white flowers, and these individual flowers do not generally self-pollinate (they are protandrous (see p36). Insects, particularly bees, move pollen from flower to flower, from head to head, and from plant to plant – watch them closely and you will see bumble bees feasting for minutes on end.

To avoid contamination with other pollen, remove any flowerheads from bolters in other varieties of onion which you are growing to eat and from shallots. Bulb onions do not cross with Welsh onions or Japanese bunching onions (*A. fistulosum*) or with ornamental Alliums or leeks. If you are growing more than one variety of onion for seed, or there are likely to be other onions flowering nearby, you will need to isolate the crop and also make sure that it is pollinated. Some gardeners bag and hand pollinate the heads, but it is much easier to isolate the plants in a mesh cage and introduce blowflies (p38-40). Commercial seed growers are now recommended to isolate different onion varieties by a minimum distance of 1000m, although distances as small as 400m have been considered acceptable for producing ordinary commercial seed in the past.

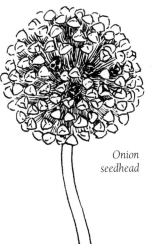

Onion seedhead

Harvesting and cleaning seed

The seed on individual flowerheads ripens over a period of time, and as it does so the seed stalk changes colour to a dry light brown. The seeds are black when ripe and can easily be seed against the silvery capsules that hold them. They shatter readily, so it is usually best to harvest

individual seedheads when the first seed in them
has turned black and begins to drop. Cut the
heads, with about 20cm of the seed stalk attached,
directly into a paper sack. Hang the sacks up, or
spread the seedheads on sheets, in a dry warm
airy place so the seeds can finish ripening.

As with leeks, much of the seed will fall out
of the capsules as they dry, or can be shaken or
rubbed out, and it can be cleaned in the same way.

Onion seed in capsules

Varieties

The late Victorian varieties **Bedfordshire Champion**, **Ailsa Craig**, and **Giant Zittau**
– or modern selections of them – are still relatively widely available, and you can also
still obtain the traditional red torpedo-shaped variety **Long Red Florence**. Other old
commercial varieties are in the Heritage Seed Library. There are few family heirloom
onions in the same way that there are heirloom peas and beans, but many gardeners
who grow for exhibition maintain their own strains for the show bench – sometimes
saving the seed of one variety for many years.

Bulb onions are thought to have originated in the area now made up by Afghanistan,
Iran and the south of the former Soviet Union, and here many more different local
strains still exist. Some of these have been taken into Heritage Collections in the US
and Europe, and have become popular with home seedsavers.

Up-to-Date

A straw-coloured globe-shaped onion, which looks similar to the still widely available
Bedfordshire Champion, but which has an important additional quality. In Ministry
of Agriculture trials in the 1940s, Up-to-Date was shown to have good resistance to
white rot disease. In the 1970s, however, the Ministry dropped the variety from the
National List as being a synonym of Bedfordshire Champion, which has little resistance
to the disease – a good illustration of how valuable genes do not always become
apparent in a superficial inspection. Up-to-Date goes back at least to the 1920s.
Harrisons of Leicester introduced it onto their list in 1928, for example, and the seed
sent to the Heritage Seed Library came originally from R. Brittan Seeds in Northampton
in the mid 1980s. Lawrence Hills once described the onion as '...the strongest yet,
bred to go with bread and cheese and realer than real ale'.

Rousham Park Hero

This onion was bred in the 1880s at Rousham Park near Bicester in Oxfordshire by
Mr Wingrove, the Head Gardener. With its large size and good quality, it became a

popular onion for exhibition, and gained an RHS Award of Merit. The variety was used both for autumn and spring sowing, and had a reputation as a good keeper. The owner of the nursery Deverill's, local to Rousham Park, which specialised in onions seems to have had excellent results from it: 'This variety secured a First Prize at my Annual Onion Show in 1897, the 12 specimens weighing 21½ pounds' he says in their 1899 catalogue. It is a semi-flat variety with a pale brown skin and mild flavour. A Ministry of Agriculture bulletin on onions in 1947 describes it as a type of the old variety White Spanish.

James Longkeeping

One of the varieties recommended to gardeners in Victorian times to take supplies of onions through until the spring, and Heritage Seed Library Guardian John Churchill finds this is still true today: 'I store then in 'ropes' in the potting shed' he says 'and it is usually late May before there are any signs of regrowth'. According to the Royal Horticultural Society journal in 1819, this was already '...a well known sort. It was raised by a market gardener of the name James several years ago in Lambeth Marsh'. It is a golden brown onion of medium size, sometimes described as 'top-shaped' – that is, it has flat shoulders and then tapers to a blunt point at the base. James Longkeeping was dropped from the National List in 1993.

Parsnip

Species: *Pastinaca sativa*
Family: *UMBELLIFERAE*

The range of distinct types of parsnips is relatively small. The main difference between varieties is usually in the length and shape of the roots, which can vary from short and bulbous to long and slender. In some, the leaves issue from a sunken hollow in the crown 1cm or more deep – a feature which gave the traditional variety Hollow Crown its name. The most troublesome disease of parsnips is canker, which can cause an extensive brown/black rot in the root, and some varieties are more susceptible than others.

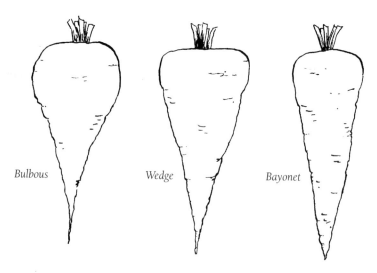

Bulbous   *Wedge*   *Bayonet*

Parsnips are an ancient European vegetable. They are very closely related to the native wild parsnip, which has similar foliage and flowers although the roots are thin, rough and stringy. Cultivated forms were grown for their sweetness and bulk long before sugar or potatoes were widely available, and they were also used for feeding stock. Some early seed lists, such as that of William Lucas in the 1670s, list the vegetable simply as 'swelling parsnep'. More selection was carried out in Victorian times to give productive types with

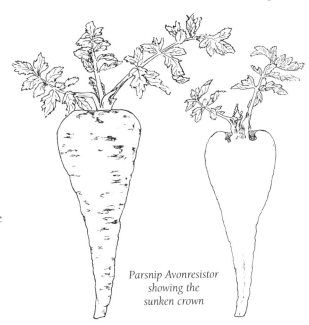

Parsnip Avonresistor showing the sunken crown

smoother skins, and the catalogues listed an increasing number of named varieties – Hollow Crown, The Student and Jersey Marrow, for example. 'In Jersey many thousands of tons of parsneps are grown annually and without his dish of parsneps a real Jerseyman would scarcely think he had dined' said Sutton & Sons' catalogue in 1863. There were also many regional varieties and right through until the 1950s and 60s some individual farmers kept their own strains.

It was not until the 1960s that more scientific breeding work began, with the main aim of producing varieties with resistance to canker. The open-pollinated variety Avonresistor bred by the then National Vegetable Research Station was one of the first to emerge from such work, and is still a favourite with gardeners today. In the 1970s work on producing F1 hybrids began. More recently, new varieties have tended to reflect supermarket requirements for small, slender, smooth-skinned and white-fleshed roots suitable for prepacking – sold not only in winter but from July until late spring.

Saving seed

Parsnips are biennial, but the roots are very hardy and easy to overwinter. This rarely causes problems to seedsavers, therefore, although cross pollination occasionally can.

Growing and roguing

Sow seed at the normal time for the variety in your area: if in doubt, wait until mid to late spring as germination can be a problem in cold soils. If you have very few seeds, you can sow them in modules in a cold frame or greenhouse to help germination; this is usually successful as long as you plant them out as soon as the fibrous roots fill the cells, before the tap roots start to form. Space the plants out and grow them on just as you would an edible crop. Pull up any roots with unhealthy foliage and any that start to bolt.

In late autumn, lift the roots and remove any that are diseased or damaged, or ones that are very forked or furrowed, and choose the best of typical shape and colour for seed saving. Parsnips are outbreeders, and it is best to save seed from as many plants as possible (see p42) – ideally at least 16. Replant these immediately, spacing them 30-60cm apart in a row or block. The alternative is to trim off the leaves to about 5cm and store the roots in a box of just moist leafmould or coir over the winter. Keep the box in a cool, rodent-free place. In early spring, replant the roots firmly.

Pollination and isolation

The flower stalks produced by parsnips can grow very tall – sometimes 2m or more – and may need staking. They produce large umbels of small yellow flowers which, as with carrots, do not generally self-pollinate. Many different insects, including bees, visit flowers and carry pollen from flower to flower and plant to plant.

To prevent unwanted cross-pollination, it is best to grow only one variety for seed each year. Others grown to eat should not generally be a problem. However, cultivated parsnips can also cross with wild parsnips, which are a common hedgerow and roadside weed in some places, particularly south east England – although they do tend to flower later. If you are in an area with wild parsnip or have other parsnips flowering nearby, then you may have to physically isolate your plants in mesh cages and introduce blowflies for pollination (see p38-40). Commercial seed growers are recommended to isolate different parsnip varieties by a minimum of 500m.

Harvesting and cleaning seed

Parsnip seed usually ripens in late summer over a period of two to three weeks. As with carrots, the seeds on the top 'primary' umbel ripen first, turning light brown and brittle. The seeds shatter readily, so check the plants regularly. If the weather is dry, harvest seed as it becomes ready by rubbing it off into a paper bag. Otherwise you can cut whole flower stems off as soon as the majority of seeds in the primary umbels are ready, and bring them in to a warm airy place to ripen and dry. Hang them in paper sacks or spread them on trays so that any seed that falls will not be lost. The seeds are very light, so sieving rather than winnowing is usually the best way to remove dust and chaff. As with carrots, the size and vigour of the seed is affected by its position on the plant – that is, whether it is from a primary or secondary umbel.

Varieties

Few gardeners save parsnips for seed, and family heirlooms and home-saved strains are rare. However, several old Victorian varieties such as **Hollow Crown**, **The Student** and **Tender and True** are still available from some catalogues. The Student, introduced in the early 1860s, is said in contemporary literature to have been bred by Professor Buckman at the Royal Agricultural College in Cirencester directly from seed from wild parsnips. He collected seed on the Cotswolds in 1847, sowed it in 1848, and by selecting plants over subsequent generations produced the variety which, according to the *Cheltenham Examiner* in 1862, '...took first prize at the International Root and Fruit show the first time that it has been exhibited'.

Mr Bound with his Bean Pea
– a home saved variety with extraordinarily large peas

Pea

Species: *Pisum sativum*
Family: *LEGUMINOSAE*

The peas in catalogues today are mostly dwarf types with white-flowers and medium-sized, deep green peas – easy to harvest commercially and good for freezing. However, in old varieties you will find some quite different characteristics: many are tall (growing 180-240cm in height), some have coloured flowers, and a few have different foliage, or pods of a different colour – purple or yellowish rather than green.

Pink/purple bicoloured flowers and small dark seeds are usually associated with field peas – the sort used as far back as Medieval times for drying and making up into 'pottage' or 'pease pudding'. However, some gardeners still grow their own coloured-flowered strains for use as fresh shelled peas. Their mealy texture and 'beany' flavour make them a quite different dish. For example, Nigel Knowlman who sent the local pink/purple flowered Forty First pea to the Seed Search wrote: 'They have a delicious taste – something between a pea and a broad bean...they taste best with fairly rich food where they provide a contrast – for example, duck with a rich gravy!!'

You might think of edible-podded peas as a recent fashion, but in fact they were also mentioned in early horticultural literature. Gerarde in his herbal of 1597 notes a group of peas 'without skins in the cods' (a 'cod' or 'peascod' is our pea pod), and not much later the term 'sugar pea' appears. The pods of edible-podded peas do not develop the parchment-like lining that gives other peas their shell-like structure, and this means that they can be eaten whole even when relatively large. Some early sugar peas did develop very large flat pods – up to 15cm long and 2.5cm wide.

Another type of pea mentioned as far back as the early 1600s is the 'Scottish', 'Tufted' or 'Crown' peas, where the upper stem joints are shortened and sometimes thickened which results in all the pods being clustered at the top of the plant. Peas with this characterisitic were once widely known, but have not appeared in commercial seed lists for many years.

A major impetus to pea breeding came in the late 18th century, when improved 'wrinkle-seeded' peas were introduced. Wrinkled seeds, so called because they shrivel when dry, contain less starch and more sugar, and are thus linked with sweet tender peas. Varieties with round seeds give less tender peas, but the plants are generally hardier. Hardiness was an important characterisitic in the days before canning and freezing, when growing an overwintering variety for an early crop was the best way of extending the season. Thus round-seeded types continued to be used in this way, and were also traditionally grown for dried peas. Most modern varieties are 'wrinkle-seeded', but some established round-seeded types remain popular for early garden sowings.

From the beginning of the 20th century, breeders were also concentrating on developing dwarf varieties. In 1897, one of the chief objectives of the seed firm Sutton & Sons was recorded as being 'to replace the small hard round-seeded tall growing sorts with peas of dwarf growth which would produce large pods full of wrinkled peas...' They certainly succeeded. A few of the best Victorian tall pea varieties such as Duke of Albany survived in catalogues until the 1960s, but by the year 2000 Alderman was the only tall podding pea on the UK National List.

Tall varieties still remain popular with gardeners, however, despite the fact that they are more trouble to support. Most give a good yield in a small space, and they can make an attractive screen, particularly varieties with coloured flowers. Victorian gardeners used pea sticks from traditional hazel coppice to stake them, but you may have to buy strong plastic pea netting or wire netting, or find a DIY alternative.

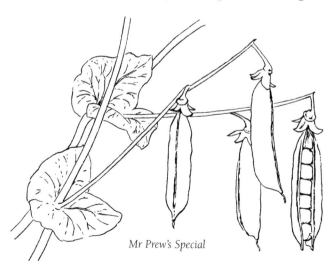

Mr Prew's Special

Mr Northover's Dorset neighbours described how he grew his tall 'mummy pea' (p25) in the front garden, on the same framework as his runner beans: 'It was quite a construction' they said 'He used to disappear inside with a chair when it was hot, to have a glass of beer or a smoke, and he picked the peas with a step ladder'.

Saving seed

Peas are very easy to save for seed. You grow
them in more or less the same way as you grow
them to eat, and generally there is little danger
of cross-pollination.

Growing and roguing

Start the seeds off as early as you can, depending on
the variety and your growing conditions. The plants
will grow best in the cool conditions early in the
season, and this allows plenty of time for the seeds
to mature and dry in late summer. Late-sown crops
often suffer from powdery mildew, which can affect
the yield and quality of the seed. If you only have a
small number of seeds, you can start them off inside
(see p33): peas can be sown individually in 3.5cm
modules or root trainers, or two or three seeds per

Pea flower – Carlin

9cm pot. When sowing direct or planting out, don't overcrowd the plants. Tall
(180cm) varieties need more room than dwarf types: space plants of these at least
7.5cm apart in a single rather than a double row. Peas are a strong inbreeding crop,
so if necessary, you can save seed from relatively few plants without affecting the
health of the variety (see p42). In general try to grow not less than five plants and
preferably 10 or more.

Make sure you know how tall the variety grows so you can provide pea sticks
or netting of sufficient height. The final height will be dependent on growing
conditions – plants may grow 30-60cm higher in wet rich soil than they do in poor
growing conditions. Pull up any plants with distorted, mottled or narrow leaves, or
any that look general weak or unhealthy – these can be symptoms of virus diseases
which are among the main seed-borne diseases of peas. Also remove any plants that
look distinctly different in flower colour, foliage or habit.

Pollination and isolation

Pea flowers usually self-pollinate just before the flowers open, so the chances
of cross-pollination are small and the isolation distances necessary are minimal.
Commercial seed growers are recommended to isolate different pea varieties by
a minimum of 20m, as much to prevent physical mixing of the seed as to prevent
cross pollination. Similarly in the garden, it is a good idea to separate different
varieties by a short distance, or by another tall crop, so that they do not become
muddled as they grow.

Harvesting and cleaning seed

Ideally, the pods should be left on the plant in the garden to dry. However, once the pods have started to turn pale brown and parchment-like, whole plants can be pulled up if necessary and brought inside to an airy place (see p44). When the pods are dry, they are ready to shell: it is usually easiest to do small amounts by hand, but they can be threshed and winnowed. David Urwin from Carmarthenshire, who grew out a purple-podded pea for the Seed Search project, beat the pods inside a pillow case with a bamboo cane and then passed the contents between plastic buckets on a breezy day to clean the seed. Edible-podded peas are more difficult to shell because the pods cling round the peas rather than springing open.

Spread the seeds out to dry further if necessary, and pick out any that are damaged or discoloured. Small holes in the seeds, often surrounded by a dusty deposit, are caused by the larva of the pea moth. The moths lay their eggs on flowering peas in mid summer and the emerging caterpillars eat into young pods to feed on the developing peas. After about a month they eat their way out of the pod to pupate in the soil, so they are usually gone by the time you pod peas for seed. The amount of damage they cause to individual peas varies, and provided you have plenty of seeds, those affected are best removed and discarded. Pea moths are most active during June and July, therefore peas sown early so that they are not in flower during this time are less likely to be affected.

Varieties

Many of the classic pea varieties bred at the end of the 19th or early 20th centuries remained in the seed catalogues for decades, and a number still appear today. Examples include the early round-seeded variety **Pilot** – given an Award of Merit by the Royal Horticultural Society in 1903 – and the wrinkle-seeded maincrop varieties **Gradus**, **Lincoln** and **Senator**. The tall podding pea **Alderman** – probably a selection of the Duke of Albany (see later) – and the tall large-podded sugar pea **Carouby de Mausanne** are also still available. Peas are very popular with home seedsavers, and many other old commercial varieties and family heirlooms have been kept in cultivation in gardens – some in the Heritage Seed Library date back over 100 years.

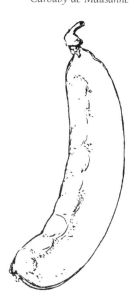

Carouby de Mausanne

Edible podded peas

Kent Blue

A dwarf variety (75-90cm) with intense pink/purple bicoloured flowers which quickly fade to blue. The small flat edible pods which follow are crisp and sweet. It is a family heirloom sent to the Seed Search project by Mr Hadow whose grandfather used to have them in his garden near Sevenoaks in Kent. 'Our family have grown them since at least the 1940s' says Mr Hadow 'They are so easy to grow'. And they are so decorative too: an ideal potager plant.

Eat All

A family heirloom sugar pea which dates back over 100 years, notable for its very large broad flat pods. Seeds were sent to the Seed Search project by Mr Symonds from Halesworth in Suffolk. 'My Grandfather told my mother that he'd grown them for over 50 years' said Mr Symonds 'He died in 1939 and we have grown them since then. We eat them just as the peas start to form in the pods, at about 2½ inches [6cm]'. When mature, the pods are often at least twice this length and as much as 3cm across. The variety has pink/purple bicoloured flowers and grows to a height of around 180cm.

Golden Sweet

This variety is distinct for its golden yellow pods, and is reputed to be one that Gregor Mendel grew back in the mid 19th century during his work on the laws of genetics. It grows vigorously to around 180cm and has bicoloured pink/purple flowers, which together with the coloured pods, make it an attractive addition to an ornamental garden. Pick the pods for eating when they are small and tender.

Shelling peas
Carlin

A drying pea associated with the north east of England, where it is traditionally eaten on Carlin Sunday, the second Sunday before Easter. Locally it is said that when the area was besieged back in the 17th century, a cargo of the peas was thrown up by a shipwreck and saved the people from starvation. Some say that the ship arrived in Newcastle in 1644, others that it was at Hartlepool or Berwick-on-Tweed. Whatever the truth of this story, the peas have certainly been grown by gardeners in the area for years. The seeds sent to the Heritage Seed Library originated from those given as a wedding present to the donor's great, great grandfather. The plants grow to 2m and have pink/purple bicoloured flowers. When dried the peas are brown and mottled. One traditional recipe is to soak them overnight, then boil them with a ham shank or bacon fat until they are soft. Their flavour is strong and earthy – not at all like the mushy peas that we eat with fish and chips today.

Purple Podded

Although the pods of these peas are a dark purple, the peas inside are green. It is a tall variety growing to 150-210cm with pink/purple bicoloured flowers. Strains of peas with purple pods were on the market as far back as the 1700s, and this particular variety was on the National List right up until 1993 before it was dropped by the seed companies and taken into the Heritage Seed Library. Other strains have been saved by gardeners, some with long family histories. For example, the strain Clarke's Beltony Blue sent to the Seed Search by Mrs Anderson of Lewes in Sussex was grown on her great grandfather's farm in County Tyrone at least as far back as the 1850s. Purple podded peas may have originally been grown for drying, but gardeners who grow them now seem to like their flavour fresh. Some say they find the coloured pods, which stand out beautifully from the green foliage, are easy to pick and less attractive to birds.

Mr Bound's Bean Pea

An extraordinarily large black-eyed pea – one of the most unusual varieties found by the Seed Search (see p22). Mr Bound who sent us the seed had been growing it for around 30 years in his Hampshire garden, and managed to trace it back as far as the 1950s when the variety was locally popular in the Whiteparish area on the Hampshire/Wiltshire border. Now he says, most of the people that grew it no longer garden or they have given up growing the pea because it is so tall. The plants can grow up to 210cm tall and produce lots of foliage and pink/purple bicoloured flowers. They can become top heavy, so give the plants plenty of space and strong supports – Mr Bound grows his up wire netting. He has always enjoyed the peas freshly cooked for their broad bean-like texture and flavour.

Mr Bound's Bean pea compared with standard sized pea

Champion of England

A tall, white-flowered pea said to be directly derived from of one of the first wrinkle-seeded peas. It was bred by William Fairbeard of Sittingbourne in Kent and introduced in 1846. The story goes that the entire stock was sold on a Sunday morning for 'a pot of beer', which seems a small price to pay for what turned out to be a much sought-after variety. The peas were considered 'unsurpassed in flavour and sweetness' by one authority in 1884 and over 100 years later Heritage Seed Library guardians agree. Harold Postings comments 'As sweet a pea as any you can grow'.

Duke of Albany

Introduced around 1882, this was one of a group of similar popular varieties characterised by their vigour, and extra long pods well-filled with large sweet peas. Duke of Albany was particularly noted for the deep colour of its pods and peas. Mrs Whitely from Hornby in Lancashire who sent the variety to the Seed Search, originally got her seeds from a local seed merchant in 1971, which must have been shortly before it was dropped from the National List. She says 'It grows very tall, to the top of 8 foot [240cm] sticks, and has deep green nearly straight pods with up to 10 peas per pod. A very very good eating pea; only needs bringing to the boil and they are cooked.'

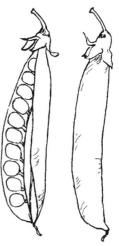

Duke of Albany

Pepper and chilli

Species: *Capsicum species*
Family: *SOLANACEAE*

Compared to what you see in the shops, the range of peppers and chillies you can grow yourself is enormously diverse. Varieties vary most noticeably in the shape and colour of the fruit, but there are also differences in plant habit, foliage and flower colour. For example, there are dwarf chillies with purple flowers and delicate cream and green variegated leaves which are as neat and decorative as any pot plant. Also important to gardeners are the variations between varieties in tolerance to cold and in resistance to disease.

The sweet peppers most commonly sold are those that are green at first and then ripen to red, but there are varieties that start greenish white, yellowish, or purple and ones that turn to bright yellow, orange or brown when mature. The various coloured pigments and the varying sugar levels in the fruit influence the flavour so, for example, red peppers usually have a different, sweeter taste than green ones. The size and shape of the fruit and also the thickness of the fruit wall will help determine how a variety is used. Thick-walled fleshy types are usually the best raw in salads, but tend to be the latest to mature and the hardest to grow in unheated greenhouses or tunnels. Commercial growers and supermarkets generally favour these types as they have a longer shelf life.

Although they are commonly thought of as long and red, chillies have an equally wide spectrum of colours and shapes, and dramatically different degrees of pungency. They may look more exotic, but they are no more difficult to grow than sweet peppers, and in fact are often more tolerant of extremes of temperature and lower fertility. The growing conditions can have some effect on the heat of the fruit, but primarily this depends on variety. There is even a special scientific unit for measuring it called the scoville, which you will occasionally see in catalogue descriptions. The mildest sweet peppers come in the range 300-660 scovilles, and the hottest chillies – the innocuous looking 'habanero' types – reach 200,000-350,000. Much of the heat is concentrated in the seed and internal pithy ribs of the fruit, so care is needed when preparing hot chillies for cooking or when saving seed (see below). As with sweet peppers, the thickness of the fruit wall can also vary between varieties – useful to know if you are intending to dry your crop, as those with thin walls are the easiest to dry successfully.

Peppers and chillies were brought back to Europe from South America by Spanish explorers in the late 15th and early 16th centuries, and they soon became part of the culture – both in southern and eastern Europe and in other parts of the world, particularly India. Although different types of peppers were described by 16th and 17th century herbalists, in northern Europe and Britain their use was limited. In early English seed lists 'capsicums' occasionally appear with the flower seeds.

In Victorian times 'chili peppers' were grown under glass, sometimes for ornament, sometimes for drying and grinding to be used as a seasoning. The large mild sweet peppers used as a vegetable and salad, which are so familiar today, were largely unknown here and have only been widely sold since the 1960s.

Recent breeding work has concentrated more on sweet peppers than chilli peppers, often aiming to produce varieties with disease resistance, particularly to virus diseases. An increasing number are F1 hybrids.

Saving seed

Peppers and chillies are fairly easy to save for seed, particularly if you only grow one variety. They take up very little space and you can often extract the seed at the same time as you use the fruit in the kitchen.

Growing and roguing

Grow the plants just as you would for eating. Peppers are largely an inbreeding crop so you should be able to maintain a variety successfully for a short time by saving seed from just two or three plants. However, it is preferable to use more. Remove any that look unhealthy or very different from the rest in leaf shape or colour, or in habit.

Pollination and isolation

The flowers of peppers and chillies will self-pollinate, the pollen often simply falling from the anthers onto the stigma. If the atmosphere is still, gently shaking the plants to dislodge the pollen may help the flowers to set. Pollination can sometimes fail in poor growing conditions – if the temperature is too cold or too hot, or the atmosphere is too dry, for example.

Although self-pollination is common, insects may also transfer pollen from flower to flower and from plant to plant. Unwanted crossing can therefore occur if you are growing more than one variety. Most pepper and chilli varieties in UK seed catalogues are of the species *Capsicum annuum* – a few may be of other *Capsicum* species such as *C. frutescens*, but it is safest to assume that all varieties are likely to cross with one another. To prevent this you can isolate plants in a mesh cage, or you can bag individual flower trusses (see p38-40). There should be no need to introduce insects or to hand pollinate. Alternatively you can keep the different varieties apart: recommended isolation distances for peppers given in the literature vary from 30m to 200m. At the Heritage Seed Library different varieties are grown in separate greenhouses or tunnels.

Harvesting and cleaning seed

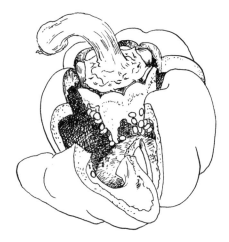

Extracting pepper seeds

The seeds are ready for harvest when the fruit has matured to its final colour – select only fruit of shape, colour and size typical of the variety. For large sweet peppers, cut the fruit wall with a knife around the stalk and down either side – the core usually comes out with all the seeds attached and it is easy to scrape them off. With smaller thinner-walled peppers and chillies some seed often sticks to the skin and has to be removed. Scrape the seeds off onto a plate or tray and leave them in a warm airy place until they are completely dry. No other cleaning is necessary. At the Heritage Seed Library, the scraping process is usually carried out inside a plastic bag to prevent the seeds shooting everywhere – they easily tip out of the bag onto a tray.

Treat hot peppers and chillies with extreme caution as the pungent substance in the pith and seeds can be harmful, especially if it gets in your eyes, and if you get it on your hands it does not wash off easily. Wear thin rubber gloves when you take out the seeds and do not touch you eyes or face (it may be wise to wear goggles). Work in a well-ventilated place as fumes are also given off.

Varieties

Up until recently, seed catalogues rarely listed more than two or three varieties of pepper or chilli, but they now contain a much greater representation of the range that exists. Traditional types from Eastern Europe and America, where peppers have long been part of the culinary tradition, are popular with home seedsavers.

Macedonian Sweet

This East European pepper variety was sent to the
Heritage Seed Library by Mr G. Twigg of Sandbach
in Cheshire. It was amongst a collection of seeds
given to him by his son-in-law's parents, who had
a smallholding near Gostava in Macedonia. 'In
Macedonia, the pepper plants are cut down and
hung to dry along the side of a barn' says Mr Twigg
'and in winter dried peppers are added whole to
casseroles.' The plants produce fairly large, pointed
sweet peppers which start green and turn to red.
A characteristic of this variety is that the green fruit
do not hang down as with many peppers, but remain
pointing upwards.

Macedonian Sweet

Sweet Banana

The plants of this variety produce a heavy crop of slender pointed peppers about 15cm
long. The fruits are green at first, ripening to banana yellow when they are ready to eat,
but they can be left on the vine to turn red. They have fairly thin walls and a sweet mild
flavour, making them popular with Heritage Seed Library members for salads or stuffing.
The variety is said to be good for containers. Grown in 20cm pots at Ryton Organic
Gardens, they make the greenhouse look like some tropical paradise and have to be
guarded from the acquisitive eyes of the chef in the restaurant.

*Julian Godfrey – a gardener at HDRA's Yalding Organic Gardens
– cleaning seed of the radish French Golden.*

Radish

Species: *Raphanus sativus*
Family: *CRUCIFERAE*

The small-rooted summer radishes, grown as curiosities by children and gap fillers by gardeners, are the most familiar type but there is far more to radishes than this! Those with large roots – both traditional hardy European radishes and the many oriental types – are far more versatile vegetables. They can be used fresh, sliced or grated; they can be stored like other winter roots or pickled; and they can be cooked in casseroles, stir fries and soups. In addition, there are some types of radish grown for their young leaves, and some grown for their fresh green seed pods.

Nevertheless, the shape and colour of the roots are usually the most important characteristics of different varieties. Both small-rooted and large-rooted types can have roots which vary in shape from long and cylindrical to flattened globes. However, whereas the small-rooted types generally have pink or white skins and are white inside, the large-rooted kinds can be much more spectacular in colour as well as in size. The skin can be green, yellow, purple or black as well as red or white and, although the giant Japanese 'mooli' radishes are typically white, some oriental varieties have coloured flesh which can range from a refreshing green to a beautiful pink or purple. The leaves of the large-rooted radishes are larger too, and tend to be much rougher and more ragged than those of the small-rooted salad types.

The 'hotness' of any radish will depend partly on variety, but it can also vary tremendously with growing conditions and with the plant's stage of growth: hotness tends to increase with the temperature and also as the plant starts to run to seed, for example. A lot of the pungency of large-rooted radishes is often in the skin, so they may be milder when peeled, and they may also loose some of their heat in storage.

Although small radishes used for their roots in summer salads, are the type usually grown by English gardeners today, this was not always the case. Large-rooted hardy types such as Black Spanish were among the first to appear in early English seed lists, and at the same time, John Evelyn's 17th century Salad Calendar recommended eating the tender young leaves of radish in early spring. The Victorians still grew the large winter radishes, and in the 1880s Vilmorin describes the Rat's Tail radish used for its pods. However, the main aim both in the large kitchen gardens and the market gardens of Victorian times was to produce 'a small and constant supply of delicately flavoured bulbs'. To this end, the gardeners used small-rooted 'forcing' or 'frame' varieties as catch crops on hot beds under glass in spring, and in cool rich moist spots in summer, and it was during this period that familiar salad varieties like French Breakfast and Scarlet Globe appeared.

Most recent breeding of small-rooted radishes has similarly been directed towards producing good all-year-round crops, with roots that do not become pithy in the centre. Some varieties have been bred specifically for growing under glass in winter, and others that will not bolt too fast in long summer days. In the last few years, some F1 hybrids have been created.

In Asia, the radish has long been a far more important crop than in the West, so it is hardly surprising that it is here where most selection has taken place over the years and where many more distinct traditional types have emerged – ones adapted to different uses, seasons, and growing conditions. The radish is still one of the most widely grown vegetables in oriental cultures, with the seedlings, leaves, stems, seedpods all valued as well as the roots. Since the 1960s, a large number of new hybrid varieties of large-rooted radish have been bred in China and Japan and some, particularly those of the long Mooli types, exported to the West.

Because radish varieties have been selected and bred for different conditions and daylengths, it is very important to sow any variety at the appropriate time of year for that variety. Sown at the wrong time, it is liable to bolt without producing an edible crop.

Saving seed

Not many gardeners save radishes for seed, although if you grow a radish for its edible seed pods, you will often find that the unpicked ones self-seed at the end of the summer. In fact the seeds are easy to collect in small quantities, but cross-pollination can be a problem.

Growing and roguing

Start off the radishes as you would for an edible crop, making sure that you are growing them at the correct season for that variety. Spring and summer radishes are annuals, and will produce seed in the same year as you sow them. Autumn and winter radishes should be treated as biennials, to give seed in the summer after sowing. Although you would normally only think of sowing radishes directly into the ground, it is often worth starting large-rooted types in modules as this makes it easier to establish them successfully. As the plants grow, discard any that look unhealthy or have foliage very different to the rest, or that bolt prematurely.

You could leave spring and summer radishes in the ground to go straight to seed, but lifting the roots once they have reached the edible stage makes it easier to select the healthiest and those most typical of the variety in size, shape and colour for seed saving. Replant them immediately, about 45cm apart, firming and watering them in well. Overwintering types must be lifted in autumn and stored like other root vegetables (p34). Replant them firmly in early spring, spacing them at least 45cm apart. There is no need to lift and replant varieties that are just grown for their edible pods; sow them as early as possible in spring and space the plants about 45cm apart.

As radishes are strong outbreeders, the more plants you have for seed-saving the better – you should have at least six, preferably 16 or more, in order to preserve the health and diversity of the variety (see p42). The plants soon put up tall stalks with many brittle branches, bearing prolific white or pink/purple flowers. Those of the large-rooted radishes can grow well over 1m tall and usually need staking.

Isolation and pollination

Radish flowers are pollinated by insects including bees and flies: they are 'self-incompatible' (see p35) which means pollen must be moved from plant to plant as well as from flower to flower, or the pods will not form. They will readily cross with other radish varieties and also with wild radish R. raphanistrum, a charlock-like weed commonly found on waste ground and roadsides.

It is therefore easiest to grow just one variety for seed in any one year, but any bolters in other varieties that you (or your neighbours) grow for eating must be removed quickly before they flower, and you cannot grow a different variety for edible pods. If you are saving more than one variety of radish for seed, or if there are other radishes or wild radish flowering nearby, plants can be isolated in a mesh cage and blowflies introduced for pollination (see p38-40). Commercial seed growers are generally recommended to isolate different radish varieties by 1000m, although where purity is less important sometimes the distance can be as little as 200m.

Seed pods –
München Bier

Harvesting and cleaning seed

When the seed pods lose their fleshiness and turn from green to brown, the seeds will be nearly ripe. The pods do not shed the seeds readily, so if weather permits, they can be left on the plants in the garden until dry and can be harvested individually. Otherwise, cut the whole branches off when the pods begin to turn, and hang them in a warm airy place to dry. Radish seed pods are dense and tough, and they must be thoroughly dry before their seed is readily released. In the early 1900s when seed was commercially produced in the UK, the radish pods were often left on the flower stalks in thatched 'stacks' in the field, or in a barn, and not threshed until the following spring.

For small quantities of home-saved seed, the pods can be crushed individually by hand and the large seeds picked out. At the Heritage Seed Library, pods are sometimes sealed inside a bag and crushed with a rolling pin, taking care not to damage the seeds, and the chaff is then removed by sieving. Seed Guardian Eddie Lancaster has his own method: he gives the pods very quick bursts in a liquidiser, and finds the seed usually drops down to the bottom out of reach of the blades. However, other seedsavers have found that this damages a high percentage of seed, so try it with caution!

Varieties

Some small-rooted Victorian radishes such as **Scarlet Globe** (1890s), **French Breakfast** (1860s), and **Long White Icicle** are still fairly readily available, along with traditional large-rooted winter storage types such as **Black Spanish Long** (see later), **Black Spanish Round**, **China Rose**, and **Violet de Gournay** which date back even further. The 19th century variety **München Bier**, which was used both for roots and pods, is also still listed in some catalogues, although in fact many of the large large-rooted overwintering radish also produce fleshy seed pods, good for eating, when left to run to flower in spring. Other old commercial varieties and a few more unusual types are in the Heritage Seed Library, but there are few if any family heirloom radishes.

Wood's Frame

A quick-maturing small-rooted radish bred in Victorian times for early sowings. It was listed by Carter's in 1845 as 'Wood's New Frame' radish and its popularity lasted for decades. (When it could no longer be described as new, it became listed as Wood's Early Frame radish.) *The Illustrated Guide for Amateur Gardeners* published in 1896 optimistically suggests sowing it in January '....on a slight hot bed, also in a cold frame, and in the open air; these three sowings will afford a useful succession if they succeed' – although in most gardens today a March sowing would stand a better chance. The radish has long pink/red tapering roots, about 5cm in length at the edible stage, and white flesh. Wood's Frame was not deleted from the National List until 1984, and has since been maintained in the Heritage Seed Library. Guardian Norma Henshaw from Dorset says 'In a polytunnel, Wood's Frame was earlier to mature than French Breakfast; a fresh clean flavour, not too hot'.

Rat's Tail

This radish, known since Victorian times, has no edible swollen root but was used for its long slender seed pods which were eaten fresh or pickled, like young radishes. Sow in early/mid spring to allow the flower stems time to develop.

Seed pods – Rats Tail

These grow to 1.2m or more with an abundance of white or purple-tinted flowers, which are followed in late summer and autumn by pods that can grow up to 25cm in length. However, they are better picked for eating when much smaller and still tender. The variety is kept by the Heritage Seed Library and in 1995 was honoured by being officially 'adopted' by HDRA's patron HRH The Prince of Wales. Guardian Mary McGee Wood says that the Rat's Tail pods have a strong, tangy peppery flavour and are good in stir fries or pickled. However, she prefers them raw in salads or sandwiches: 'To be honest' she adds 'I tend to munch them straight off the plant while I'm working in the garden, so not many get into the house!'

French Golden

A variety notable for the distinctive colour of its thick tapering roots, which have an ochre skin and white flesh. A long-standing variety in the Heritage Seed Library. Guardian Jane Gifford from County Durham sows it in early summer and says 'it usually bulks up quickly, keeping its flavour and crispness'.

Black Spanish Long

Still available from a few seed catalogues, but worth growing for its ancient ancestry. Black Spanish radishes appeared in William Lucas's seed list in the 1670s and were mentioned in contemporary horticultural literature. They were still grown in Victorian times, and the varieties available are probably little changed today. Black Spanish Long is a very hardy variety. The roots, which unlike summer radishes form entirely below ground, can grow up to 20cm long and have a thick black skin and dense white flesh. They have the reputation of being hot, but this makes them good for cooked dishes or pickles. Also try them grated as an alternative to onions in cheese sandwiches or coleslaw, or grated into a creamy sauce like horseradish.

Jane Bygott with her family heirloom variety of runner bean Black Pod

Runner bean

Species: *Phaseolus coccineus*
Family: *LEGUMINOSAE*

Runner beans provide a welcome splash of scarlet on most vegetable patches, climbing anything from a small teepee of canes to an extensive custom-built frame. There are also a few dwarf varieties, and some with different coloured flowers: white, or white and red, or occasionally salmon pink.

The habit of the plant and the colour of its flowers are two characteristics by which runner beans can be easily classified. Varieties can otherwise be difficult to distinguish, often differing only in the length, width, straightness and texture of the pod. These are qualities which have to be maintained by constant selection of the variety, and they can sometimes vary with growing conditions. Hot weather, for example, can make the beans inside the pod develop more quickly and stop it from growing longer.

The seed colour of runner beans also varies with variety. White cooked flowered varieties have white seeds, and these are the types preferred in other countries, where they are grown for the bean seeds, cooked fresh or dried, rather than for the green pods. Some UK gardeners grow white-flowered runners for the same reason – the large seeds are a good home-grown substitute for 'butter beans' (the ones you buy dried actually come from lima beans *P. lunatus*). Runner beans with bicoloured flowers have light tan seeds mottled with brown. Scarlet-flowered varieties have pale purple seeds flecked or mottled with black, although black-seeded 'sports' are common, and many gardeners have selected these over the years to produce their own strains of black-seeded runner beans. In the past, a few commercial varieties such as Black Magic (available in the 1960s) have also had black seeds

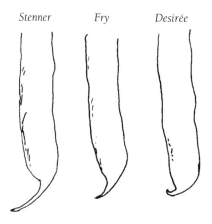

Stenner   *Fry*   *Desirée*

Runner beans nearly always have completely green pods, but some older varieties showed a tinge of red or purple, mostly down the edges. Commercially this trait has been selected out, deemed to spoil the appearance of the beans, but it still remains in some old home-saved strains, a few of which produce some very purple pods. (In climbing French beans, purple podded varieties are common – they are easily distinguished from runners by their flower colour and the way the seedling emerges (see p86). The shape and position of the point or 'beak' at the end of the pod is distinctive on some varieties.

Although runner beans are now considered a thoroughly English crop, they have a relatively short history in this country. Records show that they were grown in the 17th century, but at that time were used as ornamental plants: they probably did not flower until late August or September, when our daylength begins to match that of the mountains in Central America where they originated. When pods did form, these were probably quite short and broad. Selection over the years led to earlier flowering and fleshier pods, and by the mid 18th century 'scarlet runners' were being used as a vegetable crop.

In Victorian times they became 'the most valuable and frequently the most beautiful plant in English cottage gardens', and many family heirloom strains of runner bean date back to this time. Named varieties also began to appear in the seed lists, but although these would have been grown by the gardeners on the big country estates, a dish of runner beans was probably more likely to be served up in the servants hall than put on the dining tables of the gentry.

Along with higher yields, plant breeders have continually aimed for varieties with longer, slimmer, more fleshy pods, as have the many exhibition growers who save their own runner bean seeds. Older varieties such as Kelvedon Marvel and Painted Lady and many heirloom strains tend to have shorter pods. This does not matter to most gardeners, however, and can be an advantage because varieties with shorter pods are generally earlier to flower and crop. Kelvedon Marvel was bred in the late 1920s or early 1930s by seedsman Eric Deal of Essex, where runner beans were such a widely grown crop that every man from Kelvedon was said to have 'a runner bean in his pocket'. It still sets the benchmark by which the maturity time of modern varieties is judged.

Stringless pods are another characteristic of many modern varieties, introduced first with the variety Desiree in the late 1960s. Again, the strings on the pods of heirloom varieties doesn't seem to bother a lot of gardeners, who say they prefer the taste of these 'good old-fashioned beans'. Michael Hasshill from Liskeard in Cornwall is typical of many when he says 'Unless taken very young, when they have not really developed their full flavour, the pods do need ruthless trimming; but when they are mature enough they are crisp and tasty. I have no objection to the trimming since we have a large flock of free range hens, and they think that the cooked trimmings mixed with the morning mash are the tenderest of worms!'.

Apart from yield and long, slim pods, modern breeders are also looking for disease resistance in runner beans, and their ornamental value seems to be becoming appreciated once more. For example, the popular Victorian variety Painted Lady – also known as the York and Lancaster runner because of its scarlet and white flowers – was once in danger of being dropped from the National List, but is now widely available.

Saving seed

Runner beans are one of the most popular crops amongst home seedsavers. Provided that you have a long enough growing season, collecting seed is easy. You can take it from the plants that you are growing for eating, and the seed will almost certainly give you a good crop of pods the following year. However, maintaining a pure strain of a particular runner bean variety, with all its essential characteristics, is a lot more difficult. It will readily cross with other runner bean varieties that you or your neighbours are growing (and they are quite likely to be growing runner beans!). It will also need constant selection to keep it true to type.

Growing and roguing

Runner beans must have as long in the ground as possible if the seed is to mature, so sow them as early as you can. In cold areas, start the plants off in a greenhouse and protect them when you put them out. As runner beans are outbreeders, it is important to grow as many plants as possible to maintain the health and genetic diversity of the variety – a minimum of 20-30 if possible (p42).

Unlike French beans, runner beans are not usually grown in a greenhouse or tunnel, partly because of lack of pollinating insects, and partly because the pods will not set at high temperatures, particularly if it is hot at night (over about 14°C). However, it is possible. Eddie Lancaster grows runner beans for the Heritage Seed Library in a large glasshouse on a Northamptonshire estate: 'Once the bumblebees have found the flowers, there are no problems' he says ' The ventilation is very good and by the time the flowers are open, the vents are open all the time'.

Most seed savers grow plants for seed up strings or canes at the same spacing as a normal crop, but if you

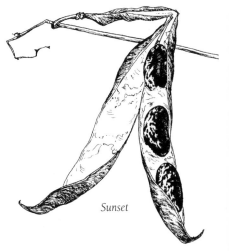

Sunset

space them further apart and limit the number of shoots, it can make roguing and selection of the best plants easier. Some exhibition growers grow plants as much as 30-45cm apart. Before flowering starts, remove any plants which look unhealthy or that have leaves very different to the rest, then as soon as the flowers open, remove any plants where the flower colour is not true to type.

Pollination and isolation

Runner bean flowers can self-pollinate, but only with outside help. Normally bumble bees and honey bees pollinate the flowers as they collect nectar and pollen. Some short-tongued bumble bees bite holes in the base of the flower and get direct access to the nectar, but usually this does not matter as other bees will use the 'correct' route to get the pollen. These will fertilise the flower, either with the plant's own pollen or pollen from neighbouring plants. Cross-pollination between plants of the same variety is desirable, but if you are to avoid cross-pollination with other varieties, you need to grow only the one variety yourself and also have an isolated garden. Commercial seed growers isolate different runner bean varieties by at least 100m, and up to1000m where purity is essential.

An alternative, if there are other runner beans varieties flowering nearby, is to somehow physically isolate the plants from insects, or to bag individual flower trusses. You then need to hand pollinate the flowers as they open. Hand pollination is a slow process, however, and a good set is not guaranteed.

The stigma and anther of runner bean flowers are coiled within a tight sheath of 'keel' petals and can be exposed by pulling gently down on the left 'wing' petal. (Bees learn to land on the left petal to give them access to the pollen and nectar.) You can then use a small soft brush to transfer the pollen from anthers to stigma – you should use pollen from another plant rather than from the same flower or plant for a good proportion of the pollinations. Afterwards relax the pressure on the wing petal gradually to allow the parts to return to the protection of the keel petals.

Harvesting and cleaning seed

As soon as pods reach the ready-to-eat stage, select ones with length, shape and colour typical of the variety for seed saving and mark them. Select only from healthy plants that are cropping well. Cut off any growth these plants make above the top of the canes, and keep the 'reject' beans well picked, together with those that form too late for seed saving. This should help the plant put its energy into seed production.

Leave the pods to mature on the plant for as long as possible in the autumn, ideally until individual pods become dry and parchment-like and can be picked off. However, once the pods start to change colour and loose their firmness, whole plants can be cut

off at the base and brought in to a warm airy frost-free place to dry. For small quantities, shell the pods by hand, and reject any seed that is shrivelled or blemished or not the true colour for the variety.

Overwintering roots

Although runner beans are grown as half-hardy annuals, they are in fact perennial plants and it is possible to overwinter the tuberous roots. These are best treated like dahlia tubers: lifted and put in a box of just moist leafmould, sand or coir in a cool frost free place, then replanted in spring. In Victorian times, this practice was recommended to gardeners as a way of getting an early crop, although advice from the seed company Sutton & Sons said that it was a 'ridiculous proceeding' and that the roots were '..comparatively worthless at best' (and, of course, it didn't help to sell seeds!).

Whether or not it gives an early crop, overwintering roots can be a useful tool for maintaining varieties. The roots will give plants that are true to type even if there have been off-types or plants of different varieties flowering nearby the preceding year. You can therefore select the typical best plants one year, and save the roots to grow on for seed in isolated conditions the following year. In the experience of Heritage Seed Library members trying this method, the same roots can only be saved for two or three years at the maximum before thay become weak.

Varieties

A few traditional varieties – or modern selections of them – are still available from some catalogues. They include the classic **Scarlet Emperor** (introduced at the turn of the 19th century), the bicoloured **Painted Lady**, and the white-flowered **Czar** (see later) – although all three have narrowly escaped being dropped in the past. The bush variety **Hammond's Dwarf Scarlet** – one of the few of this type on the market – is also said to date back to the 19th century.

Heirloom runner beans are extremely common. Even gardeners who never think of saving other vegetable seeds claim that they have never bought a runner bean seed: their stock has come from father or grandfather, uncle or aunt, or fellow allotment holder. Few are pure strains, as most are grown in gardens or on allotments where cross-pollination is almost certain to have occurred, but this does not prevent them from producing good crops of beans.

Fry

Fry

A white-seeded, white-flowered variety sold by Dobies in the 1970s, when they were an independent seed company based at Llangollen. It was said by the then National Vegetable Research Station at Wellesbourne to be not just

153

a white variant of a scarlet form, but 'quite distinct' and likely to become more widely available. Instead, it was deleted from the National List. It obviously remained popular with some gardeners, however, as more than one sample was sent to the Seed Search project. Mr Smith from Cheshire came across Fry growing in an elderly gentleman's garden in the mid 1980s. He liked the long stringless beans and since then has grown it himself and saved seed – able to keep the strain true because there are 'no other red beans about'. The variety gives a good crop of medium length, smooth, fleshy green beans, and any left to mature can be shelled for 'butter beans'. White-flowered runner beans sometimes set better than red-flowered ones in hot conditions, probably because the petals reflect the heat.

Sunset

A variety worth growing just for its beautiful salmon-pink flowers, but which also produces a good crop of medium length stringless beans. Heritage Seed Library member Joan Black grew them for years on her allotment in Aberdeen after she had been told that they did well in short growing seasons, and in the spring of 1996 was not pleased to hear that the variety was being dropped from the National List: 'I was so angry it took days to calm down!' she wrote 'Well, I had my tray of seed germinating, 40 plants growing up two wigwams and those pink flowers never looked so lovely'. Joan was one of several members who were able to supply seeds of Sunset to the Heritage Seed Library, who have maintained it since. Recently however, it has begun to reappear in seed catalogues.

Stenner

A variety selected and maintained for nearly 30 years by exhibition grower Mr Stenner (see p23), during which time it has won countless prizes for the many keen gardeners who grow it for show (several of whom sent it to the Seed Search project). Mr Stenner rogues the plants rigorously and keeps seed from only the best each year. The seeds are mottled purple and black and must, he says, have a 'lily white eye' . The plants are vigorous with scarlet flowers and produce a heavy crop of extremely long slim straight beans – consistently over 40cm long at the ready-to-eat

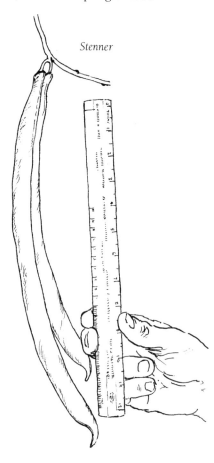

Stenner

stage. 'This bean has had so much work put into it that its bound to be different' says Mr Stenner 'It's in a class of its own for exhibition, but is also highly productive and welcome in any kitchen.'

Blackpod

A family heirloom variety, sent to the Seed Search by Jane Bygott from Shropshire. She got the beans from 'Aunt Mary', who was still growing a few plants up a trellis in the corner of her garden when she was well over 90. Aunt Mary's father, who farmed in the Bridgnorth area, grew the beans before her so, Jane says, they must go back at least 100 years. They have the mottled violet/black seeds and scarlet flowers normal for a runner bean, but the pods on many of the plants are tinged with purple when they are young and grow dark purplish black when older. Jane has been selecting to keep this characteristic over the dozen or so years that she has been growing the bean herself. The pods are fairly short (usually around 20cm) and broad with short 'beaks', but they are smooth textured with few strings.

Czar

A white-seeded, white-flowered runner bean bred in 1885 by Thomas Laxton, founder of the Bedfordshire nursery famous for raising the Royal Sovereign strawberry and the pea that bears his name. According to Lawrence Hills, the runner bean was named after Czar Alexander III, who ordered the first and only five-funnelled battleship in the world! Whatever the truth of this story, Czar was a good vigorous variety, and in 1918 was highly commended by the judges in the Royal Horticultural Society's trial of runner beans at Wisley. It has medium length pods, fairly rough in texture but mild in flavour with few strings, and if left to mature it has a reputation for giving a tasty crop of large 'butter beans'. It is still on the National List – just. It was threatened with deletion in 1988 because of the take over of the seed company Sharpes of Sleaford who maintained it. Lawrence Hills campaigned to 'Save the Czar', and won. In the following years he grew it in celebration in the garden of his bungalow at Ryton Organic Gardens.

Spinach

Species: *Spinacea oleracea*
Family: *CHENOPODIACEAE*

Several different leafy greens are commonly given the name 'spinach', both in the UK and other parts of the world, but our true spinach is the annual vegetable *Spinacea oleracea*. Spinach plants are notoriously sensitive to day-length, bolting quickly in long days, especially when conditions are hot and dry. The best crops are produced in autumn and early spring, with successive sowings to give pickings until early summer. Some gardeners grow it as a cut-and-come-again seedling crop, to give a quick harvest of small young leaves for cooking or salads. It is this quick growth and harvest of annual spinach that makes it such a vibrant vegetable, with leaves so tender and succulent that, as one 19th century writer says, '... when properly cooked [they] will be found, like the best potatoes, to have butter in them already'.

The appearance of different varieties of spinach vary mainly in the habit of the plant and the shape, size and texture of the leaves. One other distinction between different varieties used to be in the seeds: some varieties had 'prickly' seeds, with so many spines on them that they would stick to your hands and clothing, whereas others had smooth seeds. This distinction appears in the earliest seed lists: William Lucas in the 1670s lists both 'round' and 'prickly' spinach, and spinach had probably been grown for at least a century before this. Prickly seeded varieties had the reputation for being hardier, and hence were used for autumn and winter crops. The round-seeded types, which usually also had rounder and broader leaves,

Prickly spinach seed

Round spinach seed

were used for summer sowings. Although debatable, this distinction between hardy prickly and round summer spinach remained through Victorian times – when the crop was produced all year round in the kitchen gardens of the large country estates – right up until the 1950s and 60s.

Spinach is now an important crop for processing, and plant breeders have concentrated on producing varieties with an abundance of large thick fleshy leaves, and increasing the hardiness of the plants and their resistance to bolting. Varieties have also been bred with some specific resistance to downy mildew. The line between 'summer' and 'winter' spinach has become blurred and most modern varieties are dual purpose. Although prickly seeded varieties are used in breeding programmes, very nearly all, if not all new varieties produced since the 1960s and 70s have round seeds. Many are F1 hybrids.

Saving seed

Most gardeners have inadvertently let annual spinach go to flower, but few seem to collect seed – even though the relatively large amounts needed for successive sowings of cut-and-come again crops could make it well worthwhile. It is an easy crop in that seed can be produced relatively quickly, early in the year, but cross pollination can be a problem.

Growing and roguing

Sow the seeds at a suitable time for the variety that you are saving: usually early spring, but if winter hardiness is a required characteristic, sow in autumn and protect with cloches during severe winter weather. For reasons that will become apparent, it is important to sow sparsely at the final spacing and not to thin the seedlings so that you get a representative population of plants. You also need as many plants as possible – preferably at least 30. Luckily, they do not take up much space and are in the ground for a relatively short period.

As the plants grow, remove any that look unhealthy or not true-to-type. Yellow or brown patches on the upper surface of the leaves may be a symptom of downy mildew which can be seed borne. It is also essential to remove any plants which bolt much earlier that the rest without forming a good rosette of leaves, otherwise you are likely to get more early bolters in future generations.

Pollination and isolation

Spinach is unusual for a vegetable in that some plants may have only male flowers, some only female flowers, and some may be hermaphrodite (they have both). The flowers themselves are inconspicuous, but you should be able to see a difference if you look closely: female flowers cluster in the leaf axils, whilst the male flowers are

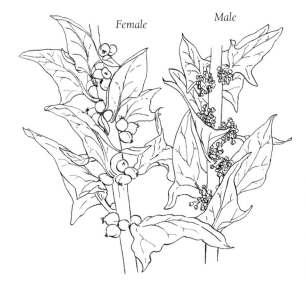

Female
Male

borne on small tassels; the male plants tend to produce fewer, smaller leaves on the flower stalks. Most traditional spinach varieties have separate male and female plants, and sometimes also plants that are hermaphrodite (the proportion of each type will depend on variety, and on growing conditions). In most new varieties, the plants are hermaphrodite. Pollen is transferred between plants by the wind.

The pollen can be wind borne over long distances, so it is easiest just to save the seed of one variety. However, bolting plants in neighbouring gardens can still be a problem. Commercial seed growers are recommended to isolate different spinach varieties by 500-1000m. As with beetroot, cages covered with insect-proof mesh will probably not be satisfactory for isolation as the pollen is very fine, although they could reduce the airflow and the probability of contamination – especially if other crops are some distance away. Horticultural fleece is more likely to prevent pollen entering, but can cause problems with humidity. Plant breeders use special pollen-proof mesh for isolating spinach.

Harvesting and cleaning seed

Leave the seeds to ripen on the plants, which will become yellow then dry. If necessary, you can bring whole plants into a dry airy place as soon as they start to become yellow and the earliest seeds are ripe, and hang them in paper sacks or spread them on sheets. This can prevent seed being dropped and lost, as well as spoilt by wet weather. Strip the seeds from the stalks by hand when they are dry – wear gloves if they are prickly.

Varieties

Some old round-seeded varieties of spinach, such as **Viroflay** (1860s) and **Bloomsdale** (1920s), are still available from catalogues if you look for them; prickly-seeded varieties are becoming harder to find. Home-saved strains are rare, but many gardeners grow and save other traditional spinach-like greens: annuals such as beetberry or strawberry spinach (*Chenopodium capitatum*), and orache or mountain spinach (*Atriplex hortensis*), for example, both of which appear in early seed lists. The plants readily self-seed, but seed is often collected too, and passed on to other gardeners.

The perennial plant commonly known as Good King Henry (*Chenopodium bonus-henricus*) is also traditionally grown as a spinach substitute, particularly in Lincolnshire where it is known as 'Lincolnshire Mercury' or 'Marcury' or sometimes 'Lincolnshire asparagus'. Ben Duncan from Tatershall, who has plants that originally came from those grown in his grandfather's garden, says '...ordinary people eat it regularly as a vegetable, mostly steamed to accompany roast meats'. It has dark green arrow-shaped leaves, and produces shoots early in spring, when there are few other leafy greens.

Neil Munro – Senior Horticulturist at HDRA's
Heritage Seed Library with the squash Lady Godiva

Squash

(including marrows, pumpkins and courgettes)

Species: *Cucurbita pepo, C. maxima, C. moschata*
Family: *CUCURBITACEAE*

The most practical way of classifying this very varied group of vegetables is as either 'summer' or 'winter' squash. Summer squashes are those eaten fresh from the plant when young and tender – often whole with the skin and immature seeds. They include courgettes and our traditional vegetable marrows as well as some more oddly shaped types: the scalloped custard marrows and crookneck squashes, for example. Many summer squashes form bushy plants, rather than long trailing vines.

Winter squash are those eaten when mature, after they have formed a hard skin, and they will often store for up to six months. The name pumpkin is usually reserved for the large round orange types that made Cinderella's coach, but winter squash come in all sorts of sizes and shapes, many of which could equally well belong in fairy tales – the Turk's Turban or giant Banana Pink, for example. Colours can range from creamy yellow through grey and green to bright orange; the skin can be smooth to touch or exceedingly warty; some fruit are small enough to be carried in the palm of the hand, whilst others need both arms and are the largest vegetable you are ever likely to produce from your garden. One of the most important qualities is the texture of the flesh – whether it is smooth or stringy, dense or watery, sweet or bland. This will determine how the variety is best used: roasted, steamed or pureed, in a savoury soup or a sweet pumpkin pie.

A few varieties double as both summer and winter squash and can be used fresh or stored. Other parts of the squash plant can be used too: the flowers can be stuffed, made into fritters, or used in salads or soups, and in Asia the tendrils and young

shoots are harvested for greens. There are also varieties whose seeds have no hard outer coat and make a ready-to-eat nutritious snack.

It would be useful for gardeners and seedsavers if these culinary categories corresponded directly to the different botanical species to which squashes belong, but unfortunately this is not the case. Although the majority of summer squashes are of the species *C. pepo* and most winter squashes grown in this country are *C. maxima*, there is some overlap, and a few varieties belong to other species entirely (eg Butternut squashes are *C. moschata*). The different species can be differentiated by the characteristics of other parts of the plant, such as the shape and hairyness of the leaves, the corkiness of the fruit stalk, and the colour of the seeds, but telling them apart is not always easy. Some of the more specialist catalogues list squash varieties by species.

The diversity of the different squashes and the uses to which they can be put are relatively new to the UK. Some types reached southern Europe from their homeland in America within a few decades of Columbus's first voyage, and the vegetables 'pompion' and 'mekin'- interpreted as pumpkin and (possibly) marrow – appear in 17th and early 18th century British seed lists. However, in Victorian times pumpkins get only a passing mention, and it was the many different varieties of marrow that were much valued as a summer vegetable: varieties such as Long Green Bush (pre 1879) and Green Trailing (pre 1885) date back to this time. 'The only gourd generally cultivated in England is the vegetable marrow, and the people do not even know the importance of the others, especially the keeping kinds grown in America and France' wrote Vilmorin in 1885.

Little changed for decades. Courgettes only began to creep in to the UK during the 1950s and 60s, although they had long been popular in France and Italy. Pumpkins were restricted to the mammoth types, prized for competitions, hollowed for halloween lanterns, but rarely valued in the kitchen. However, by 1970 F1 hybrid courgettes had appeared in garden seed catalogues, bred to give a large quantity of evenly shaped cylindrical fruit for the commercial market. More recent breeding programmes have aimed to produce varieties that have some resistance to specific diseases, particularly powdery mildew and virus diseases. Now, as the different types of winter squash become commercially popular, plant breeders are taking the same interest in these.

Saving seed

Provided you have a long enough growing season, squashes are easy to grow and harvest for seed, but there can be a great difficulties in keeping varieties pure.

Growing and roguing

Sow the seeds as you would for a crop grown to eat. Start them off in pots in a greenhouse with some heat to get an early start if possible, because the fruits need several months to grow and mature to give ripe seed. As soon as conditions permit, put the plants out at the normal spacing for that variety. Alternatively, they can be grown to maturity in a greenhouse or polytunnel if you have enough room.

It is important to grow as many plants as you can to allow for pollination between them and for roguing. Professional growers consider six plants to be the minimum for maintaining a variety, and this is normally the number grown at the Heritage Seed Library. However, although squash are outbreeders, they do not suffer too much from inbreeding depression (p42) and many home seedsavers grow just two or three plants.

Once the plants have started to grow, look out for any whose foliage is very different from the rest or which look unhealthy, and pull them up immediately. Leaves that are crumpled and/or have yellow mottling may indicate that the plant has cucumber mosaic virus, which can be seed borne.

Pollination and isolation

Squashes have separate male and female flowers on the same plant, and they are generally pollinated by bees; these move pollen between open flowers both on the same and different plants. Varieties of the same species will readily cross-pollinate over long distances. This does not usually apply to varieties of different species, but unless you are absolutely sure of their botanical classification, it is wisest to assume that all varieties that you (and your neighbours) are growing are likely to cross.

If you have an isolated garden, and are growing just one variety both for eating and for seed, you do not have to worry about unwanted cross-pollination. However, if there are other squashes flowering nearby, you will need

Tie string or ribbon round the stem of the hand-pollinated squash and mark its position with a cane.

to bag and hand pollinate individual flowers (see p41). As squash produce splendidly large flowers, this is not difficult and is usually very successful. Commercial seed growers are recommended to isolate different varieties of squash by distances of 1000m or more.

As soon as fruit begin to form, check that they look true to type. It is important that any plants bearing 'odd' fruit do not contribute to the next generation of seed. If you are bagging and hand-pollinating individual flowers, do not use flowers from these plants. If you are not, remove the plants immediately. However, seed in fruit that has already formed on the other plants may have already been contaminated.

Mark the fruit you are saving for seed, and leave them on the plant until they are mature: the skin becomes harder, and it usually changes colour. This is the stage that winter squash are picked for storing and eating, but is well beyond the normal eating stage of courgettes and other summer squash. Pick the fruit and leave them in a warm, dry airy place for the seed to finish maturing – the greenhouse staging is ideal, but they are attractive enough to be left on any sunny windowsill. A leaflet issued to commercial seed growers in 1950 suggested that 'a good test of ripeness ... is the hollow sound obtained by tapping the marrows with the knuckles', but usually it is easy enough to tell by their appearance!

After a minimum of three or four weeks, the fruit should be sufficiently ripe for you to cut them open and scrape out the seeds – for winter squash in storage, you can wait until you cut them for eating. Wash the seeds to remove any fibre. If you rub them with your hands in a bowl of water, the good seeds should sink to the bottom and any immature seeds or debris should float and can be poured away. Drain the seeds in a sieve and spread them out on a plate or tray in a warm airy place to dry.

Varieties

Some of the Victorian marrows such as **Long Green Bush** and **Long White Bush**, or modern selections of them, are still available from some catalogues, and you can also still find traditional open-pollinated courgettes from Europe amongst the F1 hybrids: **Long Cocozelle** and **Black Milan** from Italy, and the spherical **Rondo de Nice**, for example. UK family heirloom squashes and home-saved strains are rare. In France and the USA, more heritage varieties of winter squash still survive – and the recipes and tales to go with them, and some of these varieties were popular with home seedsavers in the UK long before they began to appear in mainstream seed catalogues.

Lady Godiva *(C. pepo)*

A pumpkin appropriately named for its large hulless seeds which make a tasty snack, raw or lightly roasted. The trailing plants produce medium-sized round fruit, which are green with deep yellow stripes when mature. The largest grown at the Heritage Seed Library are about 30-40cm across. The variety originates in the USA but has become a favourite amongst Heritage Seed Library members, and also with the staff – although whether this is because of the real Lady Godiva's association with Coventry or because there is an occasional excuse to taste some of the dark metallic green seeds is debatable. Many gardeners grow the variety just for the seed and find the flesh rather tough and fibrous, but others use it as a normal pumpkin in soups and curries.

Aubergine Blanche *(C. pepo)*

A summer squash originating in France. The bushy compact plants give very pale green aubergine-shaped fruit, which are about 60-75 cm long when mature. They can be cut young as a courgette or when larger – either way the flavour appears to be something special. Seed Guardian Jill Yeates did lots of taste tests to compare them with courgettes and found they had 'a milder flavour with definite flowery undertones', whilst Phillip Humphrey used his fruit when they matured and notes 'taste superb' and unlike his marrows 'retains shape well during cooking'.

Pink Banana *(C. maxima)*

An American variety dating back to 1893: a long-keeping winter squash, but certainly not a conventional pumpkin! The vigourous trailing plants bear long zeppelin-shaped fruit which can grow enormous. They are pale yellow at first but develop a pink tinge when ripe, and the flesh is vivid orange: '...the colour of tinned peaches' says Heritage Seed Library member Valerie Thorn, whose largest fruit weighed over 14kg and was 'a source of great wonder and speculation to all the other gardeners'. Judith Offord had smaller fruit, but says one was still enough for two meals: half of it was 'stuffed with mixed vegetables and cous cous, topped with parmesan cheese and baked in the oven – delicious'.

Rouge Vif d'Etampes *(C. maxima)*

A traditional French pumpkin grown there since the middle of the 19th century, and in the mid 1880s still '... the kind which is most frequently seen in the Central Market at Paris'. The mature fruit are a distinctive bright reddish orange, deeply ribbed and round – although too squashed to be Cinderella's coach or a Halloween lantern. At Ryton Organic Gardens the fruits reached 50cm or more across with no special treatment, and stood out amongst the vigorous trailing foliage to provide an eye-catching display for visitors. The flesh is light orange – ideal for the traditional French farmer's *'soupe à la citrouille'*.

*Harriet Brown with one of the
enormous fruits of the home saved tomato variety Carlton.*

Tomato

Species: *Lycopersicon lycopersicon (syn. L. esculentum), L. pimpinellifolium*
Family: *SOLANACEAE*

Tomatoes come in a great range of shapes, sizes and colours, although to look in the greengrocers or supermarket you would not think so! The colour of the fruit can vary from the standard red through orange, yellow, cream and pink to dusky purple, the final shade being a combination of the colour of the flesh and the colour of the skin. There are also fruit that are striped, and those that are still green when ripe. Fruits of different colours can make a spectacular tomato salad, whilst some purple varieties make a wonderfully dark tomato sauce.

The smallest tomatoes are the tiny 'currant'-sized ones and the largest the enormous 'beefsteaks'. In between come ones that are plum-shaped or pear-shaped, or have pronounced ridges or points. The internal structure of the fruit can vary too, from the liquid centres of the best salad tomatoes to the solid paste tomatoes, good for soups and sauces. 'Stuffing' tomatoes have solid walls and are almost hollow inside like a pepper. The acids and many other flavour components of the tomato are concentrated in the gel round the seeds, hence the blandness of most paste tomatoes when raw compared with the sweet tang of the cherry tomatoes.

The taste of a tomato therefore definitely depends on variety, but is also profoundly affected by the growing conditions and the stage at which it is picked. This is why varieties from abroad are not always as wonderful when grown in the UK as they are in the warmer climates where they originated. It is also why it is worth trying heritage and home-saved types that have been developed in conditions very different to those experienced by commercial crops today.

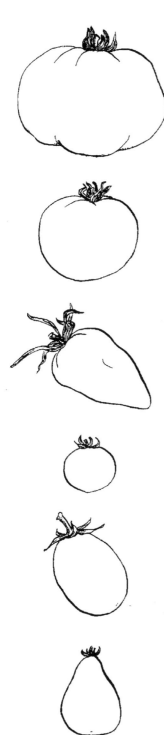

Tomato plants are generally classified as either 'determinate' (bush) or 'indeterminate' (vine or cordon). Cordon types have one main shoot which goes on growing until you – or the growing conditions – stop it. The shoots of bush types, on the other hand, stop themselves sooner or later by ending in a flower truss. However, some older, less highly bred varieties, do not fall neatly into either category.

Tomato varieties also vary in the time it takes fruit to mature and in their tolerance to cold and resistance to disease, particularly to potato blight and virus diseases. The leaf shape and size is sometimes said to affect how the plants stand up to cold, the 'potato-leaved' types with large undivided leaves being the most cold tolerant.

Only relatively recently have tomatoes become as ubiquitous in the UK as they are today. In the 17th century these 'love apples', which had recently arrived via southern Europe from Mexico, were grown only as ornamental curiosities. By the early 1800s, large red and yellow, cherry and pear-shaped love apples were beginning to appear in the vegetable sections of seed lists, but many regarded the fruit with great suspicion: it was thought to cause a 'chill to the stomach' and even cancer. Only in the last few decades of the Victorian era did the popularity of tomatoes escalate – amidst many reassurances, including one from Dr Marsden at the Cancer Hospital in Brompton. By 1880 William Iggulden, Head Gardener to the Earl of Cork, was able to write that a complete revolution was taking place. Not only were the large country house gardens growing tomatoes, but so were the owners of smaller gardens and even cottagers.

Improved varieties were selected that were better adapted to the short English summers, either for growing outdoors or under glass. Those that gave good yields of smoother rounder medium-sized fruit (preferred for salad) began to be listed in the seed catalogues, along with the large ribbed kinds and the types with small ornamental fruit that were the first to be grown. In 1895, for example, Sutton & Sons' catalogue contained over

20 red varieties including Sutton's Perfection with fruit 'round and perfectly smooth' as well as a small 'Cluster' tomato and a 'Miniature Pear-shaped....useful for dessert and decorative purposes'.

In the early decades of the 20th century, the increasing popularity of the tomato as a commercial crop, both for processing and salads, meant that not only did the new introductions have to have increased yields but also increased uniformity: '...the dreaded Moneymaker and similar varieties' as cookery writer Jane Grigson put it. Since the 1940s, plant breeders have concentrated mainly on producing bush varieties suited to mechanical harvesting, and cordon types for large scale protected cropping. Besides high yields, two of the main requirements for the bush varieties are that they must set a lot of fruit in a short period, and that the ripe fruit must be able to withstand mechanised handling – neither of which quality is generally useful to gardeners. One of the main aims in producing varieties for growing under glass or in tunnels is resistance to some of the wide range of diseases encountered in such conditions.

Both increased yields and resistance to specific diseases have been achieved by using wild species of *Lycopersicon* from Central and South America in breeding programmes in order to introduce more genetic variation. Most new varieties are now F1 hybrids – tomatoes were one of the first crops for which such varieties were developed.

Saving seed

Tomatoes are mostly very easy to save for seed and, with a few exceptions, easy to keep true to type. They are a popular crop with home seedsavers.

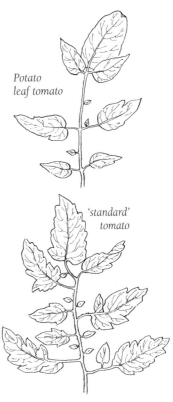

Potato leaf tomato

'standard' tomato

Growing and roguing

Start off the plants as you would for a normal crop: with some heat, in a greenhouse or on a warm windowsill. Tomatoes are inbreeders, and many seedsavers successfully maintain varieties by saving seeds from just two or three plants, but it is preferable to grow more – at least six if you can.

There is no definitive line between 'greenhouse' and 'outdoor' tomatoes. Varieties that are slow to grow and ripen do best if planted in a greenhouse or polytunnel; varieties that are hardier and quicker to ripen will grow outdoors, particularly in milder areas, but can also be grown inside. Besides increased heat, the great advantage of providing protection is that the plants are much less likely to become infected by potato blight, which can sometimes carry over in seed.

Provide strings or stakes to support cordon varieties and remove the side shoots. Bush varieties can be allowed to sprawl, although if they are growing vigorously it is best to prune them to thin out the side shoots – fruit on overcrowded plants is prone to botrytis. Some older tomato varieties behave somewhere between a bush and a cordon: they may not produce many trusses if grown as a cordon, for example, but get out of hand if left unchecked as a bush. Some seedsavers grow these varieties as multiple cordons or fans, training a limited number of well spaced shoots.

Pollination and isolation

Most tomato varieties do not cross-pollinate, partly because the flower structure makes it unlikely, and partly because the sorts of insect that usually visit the flowers are unlikely to be around. Many seedsavers find that they can grow these varieties only a few metres apart and still get pure seed. However, in some older, less highly bred varieties – particularly the small 'currant' tomatoes (*L. pimpinellifolium*) and the large-fruited 'beafsteaks' – cross-pollination is more likely. You can tell by looking at the flowers with a hand lens (see picture).

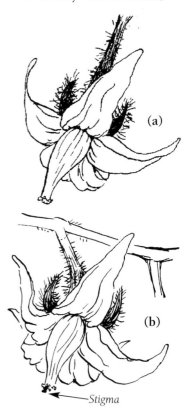

If you are growing more than one variety of this 'protruding style' type of tomato, you need to physically isolate the plants in a mesh cage, or bag individual flowers, in order to be absolutely sure of pure seed (see p38-40). The flowers will self pollinate within the cage/bag so there should be no problems with setting. Alternatively, grow the varieties as far apart as you can. Commercial seed growers are recommended to separate different tomato varieties by at least 30m.

Collecting and cleaning seed

If possible, allow the fruits to ripen fully on the plants before picking them. If not, bring the fruits indoors and ripen them as you would for eating. Cut the ripe fruit across the middle and squeeze or scrape out the seeds and surrounding gel into a jar or bowl. Note that some varieties contain many more seeds per fruit than others – and the size of the fruit is no indication of quantity. Some large beefsteak tomatoes each give only two or three

*In most modern tomato varieties, the female stigma is within a cone formed by the male anthers and the flower is almost always self-pollinated (**a**). In some older varieties, the stigma protrudes beyond the anthers and these varieties are more likely to cross (**b**).*

seeds, for example. The deseeded tomatoes can still be used for cooking, however. Heritage Seed Library Guardian David Searle finds that 'the remaining mutilated tomatoes, being seedless, make an excellent tomato concentrate'.

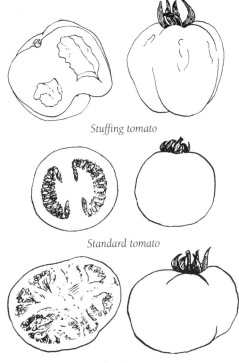

Stuffing tomato

Standard tomato

Beefsteak tomato

For large quantities of small cherry or currant tomatoes, you might find it easier to crush the whole fruit. At the Heritage Seed Library, small fruit are put into a sealable plastic bag, as much air as possible removed, and the contents crushed with a rolling pin. The pulp and skin are then removed from the seeds by flushing the contents through a series of sieves.

Some seedsavers keep small quantities of seeds by putting them directly from the fruit on to a sheet of paper or tissue. However, it is better to clean the seeds more thoroughly and remove not only any bits of flesh, but also the gelatinous layer that surrounds them (this contains a germination inhibitor that prevents the seeds sprouting inside the wet flesh of the tomato). Removing the gel not only helps stop the seeds from sticking together as they dry, but can also sometimes prevent certain diseases from being carried over in the seed. You can remove the gel either by allowing the mixture of liquid and seeds to ferment naturally, or more easily by using a solution of washing soda crystals. Some tomatoes have more gel – and are more difficult to clean – than others.

Fermentation method
Put the seeds and gel into a bowl (if there was not much gel, add up to an equal volume of water – not more – just enough to allow it to swill about). Cover the bowl containing the mixture with a cloth or loose lid and leave it in a warm place. The mixture will begin to ferment, and to look and smell really nasty! You need to leave it long enough to break down the gel, but no longer – otherwise the seed can start to germinate. Check it daily to see whether the gelatinous coat round the seeds has fermented away. At temperatures around 20-25°C the process will probably take about three days; longer at lower temperatures. When it is complete, scoop off the mould and debris from the top of the bowl. Add water to rinse the seeds, and then pour off as much as you can without losing seeds. Repeat until you have clear water with the

seeds at the bottom. Tip the seeds into a sieve, flush them through with water and pick out or press through any remnants of flesh. Then allow them to drain. Spread them in a thin layer on a tray or plate and put it in a warm airy place. Stir the seeds around as they dry to break up any clumps and help them to dry evenly.

Washing soda method

Use approximately 1 teaspoon of crystals per 250ml of water, dissolving the crystals in a little hot water and adding cold water to make up the full amount. Add approximately an equal volume of this solution to the tomato seeds and gel – coffee jars make ideal containers for this. Leave the mixture at room temperature for about 24 hours, stirring occasionally. The clean seeds should sink to the bottom. Check to see whether the gel has broken down. If not leave the mixture for longer, up to another day. When it is ready, carefully pour off the fluid and debris at the top. Add water and repeat, then clean and dry the seeds as before. This method is quicker at lower temperatures than the fermentation method, but it does have the purely cosmetic affect of darkening the seed coat. Washing soda has not as yet got official approval for seed cleaning under commercial organic standards, although it has approval for other uses in organic food production. Most non-organic commercial seed is cleaned using hydrochloric acid.

Varieties

Although there are some favourite British tomatoes from the early 20th century still around – **Harbinger** and **Ailsa Criag**, for example – many of the more unusual old varieties kept by home seedsavers have either come from America, where a much greater diversity always existed, or from southern or eastern Europe. In the last few years, some of these varieties have been appearing in UK mainstream catalogues, with companies avoiding the seed legislation by selling young plants. The Heritage Seed Library have a very large collection of old commercial and home-saved varieties, and such is the diversity of the tomato and the enthusiasm of gardeners for something completely different, that the Seed Search project discovered yet more.

Ryders Mid-Day Sun

A yellow tomato once sold by the seed company Ryders of St Albans and kept in cultivation by Mrs Joan Cullen of Friston in Sussex, who remembers her father growing the variety before her. A cordon variety with long arched trusses of small to medium-sized round fruits. Ryders catalogue for 1969 says it is 'an exceptionally early ripening variety' and Mrs Cullen has no difficulty in growing it outside along the front of her house, where she says it seems to persevere against poorish conditions. 'The yellow colour is a cheery contrast to red fruits.' says Mrs Cullen. The plants were noticeably resilient in the Seed Search polytunnel too, producing fruit well into autumn.

Carlton

A large red ribbed tomato sent to the Seed Search project by Mr Carlton of Morecambe. He had been given a plant over 25 years ago by a friend who said it was of Polish origin, and has been saving seed of the variety ever since. 'I've probably given it to 100 people' he says 'and everyone thinks it is the nicest tomato they have ever tasted. Its only fault is that its ugly!.' The plants produce some extremely large fruit, around 12cm in diameter, looking almost like small pumpkins. Mr Carlton said he produced one weighing '23 ounces' (640g) once. In Lancashire he grows the variety (a cordon) in an unheated greenhouse, and when the growing season is over the green fruit go on ripening off the plant until December.

Pop-In

A small red plum tomato, sent to the Seed Search by Mrs Hurry of Braintree in Essex. A colleague gave her a plant over 20 years ago and since then she has been saving seed because, she says, no seed company seems to sell a variety like it. The plants are grown as cordons, but sometimes the trusses need extra support: they are amazingly long and spreading, each producing a curtain of 50 or more fruit. 'The family call it a grape tomato' says Mrs Hurry 'The fruit are very sweet with a slight sharpness. Children love them as they are so easy to pop in their mouths'. In Essex she has grown the variety in both greenhouse and garden.

Kenilworth/King George

A variety grown extensively under glass by commercial growers in the Midlands until the 1960s, when it went out of favour. A number of local gardeners kept it in cultivation, however. Several samples were sent direct to the Heritage Seed Library; others were collected by the landlord of the Tiltyard Inn in Kenilworth, where there were a few regulars who still grew the variety. George Garrett, for example, got his seed from an elderly gardener who used to work at a large nursery near Kenilworth Castle where Kenilworth/King George was a popular crop: 'Just after the war, people used to walk there five or six miles from Coventry just for a pound or two of tomatoes' says George. To look at, the tomato is nothing outstanding – medium sized, red, slightly ridged, and can suffer from greenback – but, according to George, 'the taste is fabulous – taste it and you'll throw all the other varieties away.'

Sub-Arctic Plenty

A bush tomato with a reputation for hardiness and the ability to set fruit under cool conditions. It was listed by Thompson & Morgan in the 1970s and 80s, then discontinued, but judging from the enquiries to the Heritage Seed Library, the variety remained popular with gardeners. Mr Lancaster from Canterbury, who sent seed to the Seed Search, wrote that it had been recommended to him as 'the earliest tomato, said to have been developed during World War II to provide the US Air Force stationed in Greenland with fresh tomatoes.' Mr Bob Kitchin from Maidenhead, who had also been saving seed since the variety was dropped, sent us an original T&M seed packet which explains how the sparse foliage allows for quick ripening. This certainly fits in with the observations he has made on his allotment. The fruit are small (about 4cm in diameter), red and prolific, distinctive for a small point at their blossom end. Sub-Artic Plenty is now reappearing in some seed catalogues – including Thompson & Morgan's.

Potato Leaf White

One of a number of unusual coloured tomatoes from America trialled by the Heritage Seed Library in the early 1990s, and which turned out the star of the trial for its flavour and thin skin. It is a cordon variety with foliage typical of a potato-leaved tomato, and has large beefsteak type fruit which ripen to pale cream. Heritage Seed Library members generally agree on its mild, sweet taste. 'The fruit have a very ugly shape though' adds Seed Guardian Mary Eastwood – well, you can't have everything...

Earl of Edgecombe

A very large, orange beefsteak tomato sent to the Heritage Seed Library in 1995 by Cedric Baring-Gould. His great nephew Joseph Widdicombe from Millbrook in Cornwall had given him the seed and told him its story: 'When the old Earl of Edgecombe who lived near here died in the sixties, his nearest relative to take the title was a sheep farmer from New Zealand. He brought this variety over when he moved here.' Joseph thought it had since disappeared, but when Millbrook had its first horticultural show a local lady entered some of the fruit, and afterwards she gave him one for seed. The variety has since been grown by many Heritage Seed Library members. Guardian Henry Lloyd from Colwyn Bay says 'Worth growing for its colour – a bright tangerine – and very good flavour.' A cordon variety.

Turnip and swede

Species: *Brassica campestris, B. napus*
Family: *CRUCIFERAE*

These root brassicas are often considered under one heading in gardening and cookery books, although in fact they have differences which effect both how they are grown and how they are used.

Turnips can be harvested most of the year, provided you make successional sowings of types suited to the seasons. The roots vary with variety in size, shape and colour, more than most gardeners realise. They can be long and cylindrical, round and flattened, or almost globes. They can have white, red-tinted or yellow skins – some old varieties were even black – and the flesh can be white or a creamy yellow. There is also a great variation in maturity times. Varieties used for early crops can give sweet tender roots within a couple of months of sowing – a vegetable suitable for stir-fries or even grating in salads. Varieties for autumn and winter harvest take much longer to mature and are hardier; you would expect to be able to leave them in the ground into December in most areas. It is these turnips that in some recipes can be swapped with swedes, which are traditionally a hardy winter crop.

Most swede varieties are 'purple-topped', referring to the purple tinge of the root above the ground; below ground the root is creamy yellow (the extent of this colouring depending on variety), and so is the flesh inside. However, there are also a few 'green-topped' and white fleshed varieties. Swedes also vary in their tolerance to cold and in the time they take to mature: early maturing, less hardy varieties are usually harvested before Christmas; others are suited to late winter use.

As well as being useful root crops, both turnips and swedes can be grown for their leaves. 'Turnip tops' make good quick-growing 'greens' or even a seedling salad crop. Gardeners in the UK tend to grow these as a last resort – a stand-in crop after a hard winter – but in other countries they are a favourite spring vegetable. Swede roots – even those which would be too small or misshapen to cook – can be forced in the dark just like rhubarb or chicory and will give a succulent harvest of young blanched shoots.

Turnips have been grown in Britain since early times. 'This root is so well known that it needs no description...' says Culpeper in his herbal in the mid 17th century, and early seed lists offer a range of types – round turnips and long turnips, yellow turnips and white turnips. In Victorian times, they were an important field and garden crop – another vegetable that in country house kitchen gardens were expected to be available whenever the cook required. In 1863 Suttons & Son's seed catalogue offered 17 varieties of turnip (with a mere five tomatoes slotted in on the same page). Today, catalogues rarely list more than two or three – usually early varieties bred for quick crops outdoors or in tunnels – and many of the long-rooted, hardy varieties have disappeared. Some of the more recent introductions are F1 hybrids.

By comparison swedes are a newcomer, not coming to Britain from Sweden until towards the end of the 18th century. At first they were used mainly as a fodder crop, appreciated for their hardiness particularly in the north of England and Scotland. Here they began to displace turnips in winter dishes and became a popular culinary crop. In Scotland 'neeps' means swedes, not turnips. Throughout Victorian times, few varieties of swedes were on offer to gardeners, and this remained the situation right through until the 1980s: those that made it into garden catalogues were usually spin-offs from agricultural breeding programmes. Recently, however, swedes have become more fashionable as a vegetable and since the mid 1980s there has been some direct breeding of culinary varieties, aiming for qualities such as smoother skins and tender, less fibrous flesh, as well as resistance to diseases such as powdery mildew and clubroot. The more succulent their flesh, however, the more susceptible varieties are to frost damage. Traditional varieties are often hardier, and have a more pronounced peppery flavour.

Saving seed

As with leafy brassicas, it is not always easy to keep turnip and swede varieties true to type. Both crops are also biennials, although early sown turnips may behave as annuals (see later). Nevertheless, in gardens away from agricultural areas and where other swedes or turnips are harvested at the edible stage, they can be relatively easy to save for seed. The method is very similar for the two crops.

Growing and roguing

Grow swedes for seed saving just as you would for a normal autumn or winter crop of roots. As they grow, reject any plants that have leaves that look unhealthy or not true to type, or which bolt prematurely. In winter choose the best roots for seed saving, of typical shape and colour for the variety. Swedes are able to self-pollinate and are more tolerant of inbreeding than turnips, but ideally you should end up with at least six plants. They will normally be hardy enough to be left in the ground overwinter, protected with straw in extreme cold. However, they can also be lifted and stored like other root crops and replanted in early spring. Space them about 30cm apart in a row or block.

Autumn and winter varieties of turnip are grown in the same way. However, turnip varieties sown in the early spring for summer use will often go to flower in the same year. This is because, once they have taken up water, even the seeds can be triggered by low temperature into this phase. Thus it does not take much cold spring weather to make turnips behave as though they had overwintered. For these early sown varieties, it is important to choose those plants that are slow to bolt for seed saving, otherwise you will get more early bolters in future generations. Unlike swedes, turnips are self-incompatible (see p 35); two or three plants is the absolute minimum for any seed to set and you need many more – ideally 20 to 30 – in order to maintain the variation and health of the variety.

Pollination and isolation

Both crops readily cross pollinate. Turnips (*B. campestris*) will not only cross with other turnip varieties, but with other crops of the same species: Chinese cabbages and pak choi, agricultural turnips and turnip rapes. Similarly swedes (*B. napus*) will cross with other garden swedes, and also some kales, agricultural swedes and rapes of the same species. In addition, swedes will often cross equally readily with turnips and its related crops, and *vice versa*. Neither will cross with leafy brassicas (*B. oleracea*), however. The pollen is usually carried by insects including bees, although sometimes by the wind, and for commercial seed growers these crops have a recommended isolation distance of 1000m.

If there are no other potentially cross-pollinating crops flowering nearby, the plants can be allowed to flower freely and will be visited by many insects. Otherwise, to prevent contamination, the plants can be isolated inside a mesh cage and blowflies introduced for pollination (see p38-40). Any odd plants that have flowers of different colour to the rest should be removed immediately.

Harvesting and cleaning seed

As with leafy brassicas, the seed stalk and pods of swedes and turnips begin to turn brown as the seed matures, and the seeds are harvested, dried and cleaned in the same way as for these crops (see p97).

Varieties

A number of traditional turnip varieties and a few swedes are still fairly readily available. The turnips **Snowball**, **Veitch's Red Globe**, and **Golden Ball**, for example, all of which date back to the mid 1800s. Snowball is a quick-growing variety; Golden Ball and Veitch's Red Globe are maincrop varieties: 'One of the handsomest and best turnips for autumn use' said the report of the Royal Horticultural Society of Red Globe in 1877. The swede **Champion Purple Top** dates back to the mid 1800s, and **Devon Champion** is another traditional purple top variety bred, probably in the 1930s, by the seed company Tucker & Sons of Newton Abbott.

Few UK gardeners save strains of either swedes or turnips – although there are exceptions. Alec Donaldson kept the long-rooted commercial variety **Laird's Victory** growing in his garden from the end of the war right up until the early 1990s, saving seed and – since he had once been in the seed trade – cleaning, polishing and grading it. When he died, the family cleared his house and threw out the seed, but the neighbours sent the turnips that had been in the garden to the Heritage Seed Library. In Scandinavia many more local and commercial varieties of swedes and turnips have survived and have been taken into heritage collections.

*Rowan Brearley – one of the children taking part in the Beanstalk Project
with some pods of the Crimson Flowered broad bean.*

Community seed saving

Growing old vegetable varieties and saving seed has a lot to offer school projects and community groups, as examples around the country already show. In schools it can provide a practical peg for a range of subjects – botany, geography, history, maths – and a down-to-earth example for understanding what is meant by 'biodiversity' and 'sustainability'. In local communities, seed saving can link people together in a way that not only revives the taste for regional vegetable varieties, but can also save them money and be a lot of fun. Such projects often fit in well with Local Agenda 21 initiatives, the government commitment to build a sustainable society for the 21st century.

Some of the projects that have already taken up the theme are one-off events, like the aptly named 'Multiplication Table' which was organised by a Birmingham Allotment group on the day of their 50th anniversary celebration. In one shed on the site, seeds were swapped and a giant mathematical calculation performed to show just what impact this distribution of seeds would have.

Teacher Fiona Ramsell focused on 'beans and biodiversity' when she organised a project for Birmingham schools' Year of the Environment. The children grew and compared a range of varieties of beans, which came from different commercial catalogues and from the Heritage Seed Library. On one level they compared simply the appearance of the beans, how they grew, and what they tasted like. On another, they considered the environmental implications – where the beans came from and which ones were endangered – and they saved the seed. Fiona sent out 450 packs of 40 seeds to a large proportion of Birmingham's schools. 'It is likely that 15 to 18 *thousand* children took part in this project' she said 'Can you just imagine that many beans growing?'.

Back garden seed saving

Similarly Alistair Cruickshank, a former senior civil servant with MAFF, introduced the idea of old and threatened varieties of vegetable to his local 'Beanstalk Project'. This is a scheme aimed at getting unused allotments in the area into cultivation as part of local Agenda 21. The allotments are offered free to groups of children with adults – family groups, or ones from schools or clubs – and the groups are taught by experienced gardeners how to grow food organically. This year, each group had the chance to grow varieties from the Heritage Seed Library and to understand the problems in keeping them in cultivation. 'Some of the kids are in their fourth growing season now' says Mr Cruickshank 'so we reckon they are really committed'. He hopes that the project is laying the foundation for a new generation of seed savers.

Involving more local gardeners in seed saving was one of Peter Andrews' main aims when he started up Bath and Avon Seed Savers (BASS). In launching the group in Bath, he had two advantages: first, there is a local variety of lettuce, the Bath Cos; and second Bath has a large annual flower show. Peter reckoned that a stand at the show with a large 'WANTED SEED SAVERS' poster, and featuring the Bath Cos lettuce, would be bound to get the attention of local gardeners and the media – and it did.

Besides introducing gardeners to the whole idea of heritage varieties and their preservation, BASS is anxious to demonstrate that seed saving can be a social activity, and that it can also save money. 'Why, when the family and neighbours are sick to death of eating broad beans, and the freezer is full past sensibility, does the average gardener oik the plants out of the ground and chuck them on the compost heap?' asks Peter ' It is like throwing money away'. Much more sensible to leave some of the best pods on the plant and save seed to sow next year – and a few extra to bring to BASS's annual seed swap, of course.

BASS members receive two newsheets a year, which include seasonal tips on seed saving, and an invitation to the 'annual general seed swapping party' in early spring where members meet, drink tea, eat cake, swap seeds and ideas, drink more tea and eat more cake... Peter Andrews has the following advice for other would be seed swap groups:

- Gather together allies and write down what you hope to achieve
  – the organisation's aims.
- From this produce a newsletter/fact sheet .
- Try to find a 'hook' for the organisation (like the Bath Cos lettuce).
- Organise a launch event – either at another relevant local event, e.g. flower or produce show, or organise a meeting – have someone to talk on the subject and explain what you hope to achieve.
- Make sure you get maximum publicity, by sending notices to local allotments and gardening groups, and by giving a story based on your 'hook' to the local press and TV.

- Once the group is running, use a newsletter to keep in touch and make sure your members are using viable seed saving techniques – point out which crops are the easiest to save.
- Organise an annual seed swap in spring, making it a major social occasion. A plant swap day later in the year might also be a good idea.

Bath & Avon Seed Savers has been running for four years now. It has given away many packets of Bath Cos lettuce; discovered local gardeners already saving seeds; and introduced the idea to many more. Their formula that could work well in other places, particularly if you gather together allies: seed saving groups have many aims in common with other local groups, such as wildlife trusts, community orchards and organic gardening groups.

How easy is it to save seed?

This varies for each crop, depending on a number of factors. How easy is it to get the plants to the flowering and seeding stage in the first place? How easy is it to keep varieties true to type? How easy is it to finally collect and clean the seed? Your situation can make a difference too. If you have a small garden, for example, crops which need a lot of space for a long time before they seed are a problem; if you have a spare allotment, however, they are not. Conversely, if the garden is in the middle of a town and no-one else on the block grows any vegetables, crops that cross pollinate will not be a problem. On an allotment or in a garden in an agricultural area, however, it may be difficult to keep them true to type.

The table shown can therefore only be a rough guide, but in general, the crops with the low numbers are easiest to grow and those with the high numbers, the most difficult. Thus in the various columns:

Annual: 4 Crops that need a long growing seaon or some protection in order to produce seed. 1 Crops that easily produce seed outside in most seasons.

Biennial: 4 Crops that are difficult to overwinter. (1)2 Crops that are a bit more trouble e.g. Crops that usually need lifting or storing, or otherwise protecting. 1 Crops that often overwinter in the ground with no protection.

Space: 4 Crops for which you need lots of plants/space. 1 Crops for which you need only a small number of plants/small space.

Cross-pollination: 4 Crops which cross pollinate readily. 1 Crops which nearly always self pollinate.

Isolation: 4 Difficult e.g large isolation distance needed/ not easy to cage and use insects or hand pollinate. The difficulty does depend, however, on whether other varieties of the crops are likely to be flowering nearby. With biennials such as carrots and parsnips that are normally harvested in the first year, this may be unlikely.
2 Moderate e.g. short isolation distances or can be caged and will self-pollinate
1 Easy – only very short isolation distances necessary.

Harvest/clean: 4 Seed difficult to collect and clean. 1 Seed easy to collect and clean.

Crop	Annual	Biennial	Space	Cross pollination	Isolation	Harvest/ clean
Aubergine	3	–	1	2	2	1
Beetroot	–	3	3	4	4	2
Broad bean	1	–	2	3	4	1
Broccoli, winter	–	1	4	4	3	2
Brussels sprout	–	1	4	4	3	2
Cabbage, spring	–	1	4	4	3	2
Cabbage, summer	–	3	3	4	3	2
Cabbage, winter	–	1	3	4	3	2
Carrot	–	2	2	4	3	3
Cauliflower, summer	–	4	4	4	3	2
Cauliflower, winter	–	3	4	4	3	2
Celery	–	4	2	4	3	4
Celeriac	–	2	2	4	3	4
Cucumber, g/house	3	–	2	4	2	2
Cucumber ridge	2	–	2	4	2	2
French bean	2	–	1	1	1	1
Kale	–	1	4	4	3	2
Kohl rabi	–	3	2	4	3	2
Leek	–	1	2	4	3	3
Lettuce	4	–	1	1	1	3
Melon	4	–	2	4	2	2
Onion	–	3	2	4	3	3
Parsnip	–	1	2	4	3	3
Pea	1	–	1	1	1	1
Pepper	3	–	1	2	2	1
Radish	2	–	2	4	3	3
Runner bean	3	–	3	4	4	1
Spinach	1	–	2	4	4	3
Squash	2	–	2	4	2	2
Swede	–	2	3	4	3	2
Sweetcorn	4	–	4	4	4	2
Tomato	2	–	1	2	1	2
Turnip	–	2	2	4	3	2

Index of varieties

Glossary

Annual: An annual plant grows from seed, flowers, produces seed and dies all within one year; e.g. peas, lettuces.

Biennial: A biennial plant takes two growing seasons, with a cold season in between, to flower, produce seed, then die; e.g. carrots, beetroot.

Cotyledons: The first leaves of the plant within the seed that are used as a food supply for the germinating embryo.

Cultivar: Any variety produced by horticultural or agricultural techniques and not normally found in natural populations.

EC Common Catalogue: see National List.

F1 hybrid: A crop variety that is produced by crossing two selected parent varieties, which have usually been inbred to make them uniform. F1 hybrid plants can combine the qualities of the parent lines and have hybrid vigour, but seed collected from them does not come true-to-type.

Heirloom variety: A home-saved variety which people pass down from generation to generation.

Hermaphrodite: Both male and female reproductive parts present in the same flower.

Horticultural fleece: Semi-transparent non-woven material made from polypropylene, used by gardeners and growers to protect plants from frost and pests.

Inbreed: To fertilise a plant with its own pollen.

Inbreeder: A variety or species that usually naturally self-pollinates.

Inbreeding depression: The loss of vigour and genetic variability in a variety associated with inbreeding; it is caused when too few plants of a naturally outbreeding variety are chosen for seed saving.

Landrace: A primitive cultivar that has been selected by farmers and smallholders but that has not been subject to intensive plant breeding. Landraces are more variable than varieties that reach the catalogues, with individual plants often differing in appearance, harvest time and disease resistance.

Modules: Trays divided into individual cells, used for plant raising.

National List: The official list of vegetable varieties for a country within the European Union, first compiled for the UK in 1973; to be put on the list a variety has to be tested by the Plant Variety Rights Office. The National Lists of all the countries together form the EC Common Catalogue, and it is illegal to sell seeds of a variety not in this catalogue.

Open-pollinated variety: A variety that breeds true from seed: 'open-pollinated' because seed is produced by allowing a natural flow of pollen between different plants of the same variety.

Outbreeder: A variety or species that usually naturally cross-pollinates.

Parthenocarpic: Production of fruit without setting of seeds. A parthenocarpic fruit forms without fertilisation of its ovules; therefore pollination does not need to have occurred and the fruit does not contain seeds - as in some cucumbers for example.

Perennial: A plant that lives for more than two years e.g. asparagus, globe artichokes.

Protandrous: A flower is protandrous if its pollen is released from the anthers before the stigma in the same flower becomes receptive, so that it usually will not self-pollinate even if it is not self-incompatible.

Pollen: Tiny spores produced by the male parts of a flower which carry genetic information from the plant.

Pollination: The transfer of pollen from the male reproductive organs to the female; in seed plants this involves the transfer from the anthers to the stigma.

Roguing: Removing plants, the 'rogues', that you do not want to contribute to a seed crop; they may be diseased, weak, early bolters, or not true-to-type, for example,.

Seed Guardian: A member of HDRA's Heritage Seed Library who undertakes to grow a specific vegetable variety from the collection and return the seed, ensuring it is true to type.

Self-incompatible: A plant or flower is self-incompatible when it is unable to fertilise itself.

Species: A population of plants that can interbreed in nature. In general, plants which belong to different species cannot interbreed to give fertile offspring. The second part of the Latin name of a plant indicates its species.

Stigma: The receptive female part of the flower which provides the surface on which the male pollen is received at pollination and on which the pollen grain germinates.

Synonym: A variety that is the same as another variety which has a different name.

True-to-type: a variety is true-to-type when the offspring grown from seed have the same characteristics as the parent plant which produced the seed.

Umbel: A cluster of flowers spread out on stalks, which makes the cluster look like an umbrella: parsnips, carrots and many herbs have flowers that form umbels.

Variety: A distinct variant of a species, subordinate to it, either arising naturally or in cultivation. Varieties occurring in cultivation are sometimes called cultivars, although these terms are often used interchangeably.

Winnowing: Separating clean, dry seed from the pieces of seed capsule and other debris by using a current of air.

Useful addresses

Seed Companies

Seed companies mentioned in the text, or offering a good range of heritage and traditional open-pollinated vegetable varieties:

Edwin Tucker & Sons Ltd, Brewery Meadow, Stonepark, Ashburton, Newton Abbot, Devon. Tel: 01364 652403. Fax: 01364 654300.
Ferme de Sainte Marthe, P.O. Box 358, Walton, Surrey KT12 4YX. Tel: 01932 266630. Fax: 01932 252707.
Future Foods, P.O. Box 1564, Wedmore, Somerset BS28 4DP. Tel/Fax: 01934 713623. email: enquiries@futurefoods.com
Kings Seeds, Monks Farm, Kelvedon, Colchester, Essex CO5 9PG. Tel: 01376 570000. Fax: 01376 571189.
Seeds-by-Size, 45 Crouchfield, Hemel Hempstead, Hertfordshire HP1 1PA. Tel: 01442 251458. email: john-robert-size@seeds-by-size.co.uk.
Simpson's Seeds, 27 Meadowbrook, Old Oxted, Surrey RH8 9LT. Tel/Fax: 01883 715242.
The Organic Gardening Catalogue, Riverdene Business Park, Molesey Road, Hersham, Surrey KT12 4RG. Tel: 01932 253666. Fax: 01932 252707. email: chaseorg@aol.com.
Thomas Etty Esq., 45 Forde Avenue, Bromley, Kent BR1 3EU. Tel: 020 8466 6785. email: ray.warner@tometty.freeserve.co.uk
Terre de Semences, Ripple Farm, Crundale, Canterbury, Kent CT4 7EB. Tel: 0966 448379
W. Robinson & Sons Ltd, Sunny Bank, Forton, Nr Preston, Lancashire PR3 0BN. Tel: 01524 791210. Fax: 01524 791933.

Other suppliers

Many of the seed catalogues sell some horticultural fleece and netting suitable for isolation cages, but a large range is supplied by:

Agralan Ltd, The Old Brickyard, Ashton Keynes, Swindon, Wiltshire SN6 6QR. Tel: 01285 860015. Fax: 01285 860056. email: agralan@cybermail.uk.com.

Suppliers of silica gel for seed drying and storage:
Philip Harris Education, Novara Group Ltd, Novara House, Excelsior Road, Ashby de la Zouch, Leicestershire LE65 1NG. Tel: 0870 6000 193

Bibliography

Breed your own Vegetable Varieties *
Carol Deppe, 1993, Little, Brown & Company
Written for the US, but relevant for the UK too. Explains the basics of plant breeding clearly and in a very readable way, with the aim of allowing you to breed and maintain your own strains of vegetables.

Cool Green Leaves and Red Hot Peppers * - Growing and cooking for taste
Christine McFadden and *Michael Michaud*,1998, Frances Lincoln
A grow and cook book which appreciates the differences between vegetable varieties. Many useful snippets of information about how crops grow and their nutritional value.

Heirloom Vegetable Gardening * - A master gardener's guide to planting, seed saving and culural history. *William Woys Weaver*, 1997, Henry Holt and Company American emphasis but a very good guide.

Heritage Vegetables *
Sue Stickland, 1998, Gaia Books Ltd
A wider view of why our vegetable heritage is so important, why it has been lost, and what seed saving groups worldwide are doing about it. Stunning colour pictures.

Jane Grigson's Vegetable Book
Jane Grigson, 1978, Penguin books [out of print]
A vegetable cookery book, but full of history, anecdotes and traditional recipes.

The New Seed Starters Handbook *
N. Bubel 1998 Rodale Press (USA)
Good information on the techniques of growing from seed.

Organic Gardening *
P. Pears and S. Stickland 1999 Royal Horticultural Society
All the key techiques for gardening organically.

Organic Tomatoes – The Inside Story *
Terry Marshall 1999 Harris Associates
All you need to know about the cultivation of tomatoes.

Perfect Pumpkin *
G. Demerow 1997 Storey Publishing (USA)
Pumpkin and squash growing with recipes, storage tips and craft ideas.

Roots of Vegetables
Ray Warner, 1997, Thomas Etty Esq (see address under seed companies)
The history of many old vegetable varieties, with text extracted from contemporary books and catalogues.

Salads for Small Gardens *
Joy Larkcom, 1995, Hamlyn
Best book available on growing 'salad' crops. Officially out of print but stocks held at eco-logic books.

The Seed Savers Handbook *
Jeremy Cherfas, Michele & Jude Fanton, 1996 eco-logic books
Good sections on the politics and environmental reasons for seed saving. Includes seed saving details of 80 herbs and vegetables, including some unusual crops not covered in Back Garden Seed Saving.

The Seed Search *
Compiled, edited and published by Karen Platt (regularly updated).
A comprehensive directory of seed catalogue entries to help you to find a supplier for the variety you are looking for. Includes vegetables as well as flowers, shrubs and trees.

Seed to Seed *
Suzanne Ashworth, 1991, Seed Savers Publications, USA
Seed Saving guide written for the US. Includes a large range of vegetable crops.

The Vegetable Garden *
M.Vilmorin-Andrieux, 1992 (first published 1885), Ten Speed Press
Describes the varieties then in cultivation in meticulous detail, together with growing techniques and comments, giving a valuable insight into the horticultural scene at the time.

The Victorian Garden Catalogue
Introduction by Daphne Ledward, 1995, Studio Editions
Reprints of pages from the 19th century catalogues of well-known seed suppliers. A large section on those relevant to the kitchen garden.

* These books can be purchased mail order from eco-logic books.

Acknowledgements

This book could not have been written without all the committed gardeners who sent in seeds, stories and photos; filled in forms and record sheets; and were so willing to share their experiences with us. They include Heritage Seed Library Members and Guardians, Seed Donors and Seedsavers for the Seed Search project, and others who simply to wrote in response to articles in the press. It is impossible to thank them all individually, but I hope that they will recognise their seed-saving tips, family tales, and old favourite varieties in print and know that by becoming involved, they have helped other gardeners to enjoy them too.

A special mention should go to Alistair Cruikshank, Fiona Ramsell, and Peter Andrews for supplying us with information about their local seed-saving groups and projects, and to my local gardening volunteers, particularly Jan Peters and Dave Chester-Master, who helped me with my growing and seed saving, and never complained at being asked to stop and measure this, taste that, or hold something else so that it could be photographed.

Much of the rest of the credit must go to all the staff, past and present, of the Heritage Seed Library, whose knowledge of seed saving and old varieties formed the backbone to the book. Special thanks to the Curator Louise Daugherty and Senior Horticulturist Neil Munro – and to HDRA's Head of Horticulture Bob Sherman – for taking time to read through the text and for their helpful comments.

Whilst the book primarily puts forward gardener's experiences, seed saving and genetic conservation have a scientific base, and I would like to thank the following for their invaluable technical help: Mike Ambrose from the John Innes Centre, Peter Crisp of Crisp Innovar Ltd, Brian Haynes and Phillip Miller from Kings Seeds, Peter Dawson and Steve Winterbottom from Tozer's Seeds, Dave Astley and Angela Pinnegar from the Vegetable Gene Bank at HRI Wellesbourne, Dr D.A. Bond and Mr G. R. A. Crofton. Thanks also to the professional gardeners and writers Joy Larkcom, Michael Michaud, and Peter Blackburne-Maze for their advice, and to Ray Warner of Thomas Etty Esq., Robert Flood, and Marian Peacock-Pochin for their research into the archives.

The Seed Search project was supported by the Department of Environment, Transport, and the Regions.

Thank you...

Many thanks to the following people who donated or saved seeds for the Seed Search project:

Mrs Marilyn Abdulla
Mr & Mrs Ackland
M.W. Ainge
Wendy Allen
Mrs S. Anderson
Jane Anger
Liza Antrim
Natasha Arthur
Chris Austin
Colin Baird
S. Bethell
D.C. Bland
Mrs Booker
B. Bound
Val Bourne
Keith Boxall
M.H. Briers
Albert Briggs
Norman Brooks
C & P Brown
Wendy Brown
Helena Buchanan
W.H. Bull
Mrs Dinah Butler
Mrs P.J. Bygott
William C. Carlton
Jonathon Cary
R.J. Catchpole
Peter Chadwick
Olivia Chandler
F. Clark
Richard Clark
J.A. Collett
M. Cooke
Ms J.M. Cullen
Mrs A. Cummings
Mrs Rita Damper

Paul Davies
F.E. De'Ath
Sarah Dean
Martin Diment
Ben Duncan
Michael Dunwell
K.F. Durman
Mrs M.E. Fardell
Mike Fellows
Peter Feltham
Guli Field
Mr G.A. Fisher
James Fletcher
Mrs Valerie Fordham
Mrs M. Francis
Mary Frings
David Frith
P.J. Fry
Miss J. Gallaccio
Paul
and Lesley Gates
M.R. Goodall
R.J.Goulding
Samantha Green
Greenfingers Grp
Gary Grief
J. Hadow
Peter Handy
Iris Hannaford
Marie Hardie
Michael Hasshill
Isobel Havercroft
B.T. Helps
Mrs R. Hemington
Bruce Holmes
Mrs M.A. How
Ian & Linda Howell

Mrs V. Hurry
Peter Jones
Mrs B.J. Kelly
Robert Kendall
Nigel Knowlman
D.W. Lancaster
Joy Larkcom
Roy Lemmon
Graham Long
Katie Long
Mrs Katie Long
Rosanna Loveday
Peter Loveridge
D.G. Loxley
Brian Mannering
Mrs Mary Manning
Mrs Eileen Mignot
Eric Mills
Mrs Monan
Mr & Mrs M.
Morgan
Dr Valerie Muir
Mr & Mrs J.S. Muir
Mrs M. Nowell-Smith
Alec Nunn
Michael O'Connor
Toodie Ottaway
Ms Doreen May
Owen
Steve Oxbrow
Tania Percy-Bell
Geraldine Perriam
Jan Peters
R.D. Phillips
Helen Porter
Prof H.C. Prentice
Mrs G. Quirk

Betty Rackham
Miss H Randerson
June Renwick
Mrs M. Richardson
Brian Rodmell
Jennifer Russell
Mrs M.F. Seeley
Mrs M. Shuker
Mark Simmons
Richard Simpson
Dilys Skilleter
R. Skingley
Chris Smith
W.R. Smith
Brigid
& Richard Smyth
Carol Southgate
Mrs G. Sowerby
B.G. Stenner
Tony Strassen
J. Symonds
Dr Rachel Thomas
Mrs R.J. Underwood
David Urwin
Peter
and Jean Vincent
Katrina Warren
Vicki Warwick
A.J. Wastell
Adam Waterman
Alison Weir
Jill Whiteford
Mrs L.M. Whiteley
Mrs J.M. Withers

Sincere apologies to anyone we have left out.

HDRA The Organic Organisation
Back Garden Seed Saving

HDRA, a registered charity, is the organic gardening organisation, with tens of thousands of enthusiastic members all over the world.

The association runs three organic display gardens, open to the public, at Ryton Organic Gardens near Coventry in Warwickshire, Yalding Organic Gardens near Maidstone in Kent, and Audley End Organic Kitchen Garden near Saffron Walden in Essex. The gardens, with their associated shops and restaurants, win many awards and are popular tourist attractions. They are worth visiting as beautiful gardens in their own right, with many ornamental features. They also tell the story of environmentally friendly, conservation orientated organic gardening principles, in an interesting and imaginative way.

Ryton Organic Gardens is HDRA's headquarters, from where the organisations many and various activities are co-ordinated. These include carrying out scientific research into organic horticulture, providing organic information and advice to its members and others, producing a wide range of books, booklets and leaflets, working with farmers in developing countries, running an organic gardening and landscape design consultancy, a waste resources consultancy, and last, but not least, home to the Heritage Seed Library (HSL). The Library saves old and unusual vegetables from extinction and then makes them available to HSL members. This keeps them in circulation, so that these wonderful varieties can be grown and enjoyed by anyone and everyone.

Further information about organic gardening,
HDRA and the Heritage Seed Library can be obtained from:

**HDRA,
Ryton Organic Gardens,
Coventry, CV8 3LG
Telephone: 024 7630 3517 or email: enquiry@hdra.org.uk**

Alternatively details can be found on their website: www.hdra.org.uk.

A free information pack including details
of how to join is sent, free of charge, on request.

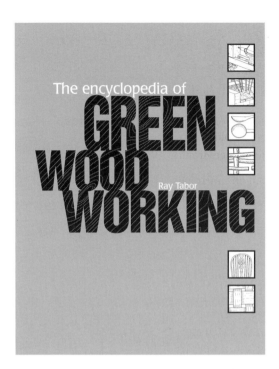

The encyclopedia of Green Woodworking

Green woodworking is a natural way of working with unseasoned wood to create a huge variety of useful and attractive products. In the past, many of the products in our homes were handmade by craftsmen working with material taken from local woods and forests. In this book Ray Tabor passes on the 25 years of skill and knowledge he has acquired as a woodsman and green woodworker producing traditional products.

Contents include: The Nature & Properties of Wood – Creating and Maintaining your own Woodland – Choosing your Wood – Tools and Devices – Patterns and Gauges – The Key Skills – Fuel – Fencing & Hurdles – Lathes and Turnery – Baskets – Walking Sticks – Spoons – Benches, Stools & Chairs – Garden Furniture.

Nothing combines natural beauty and usefulness more than a Windsor chair or a rustic garden fence made from green wood. You can use the instructions in this immensely practical and well illustrated book to create a host of useful and attractive products for home and garden.

From acorn to zale – an indispensable resource for the seasoned woodworker and beginner alike.

To purchase your own copy of The encyclopedia of Green Woodworking send a cheque for £16.95 (includes p&p) to eco-logic books.

eco-logic books

eco-logic books is a small, ethically run company that specialises in publishing and distributing books and other material that promote practical solutions to environmental problems.

Those books that are still in print and mentioned in the Bibliography plus many others are available from our comprehensive catalogue. Other topics covered in the catalogue include:

Gardening
Permaculture
Composting
Self Reliance
Food & Related Issues
Keeping Hens & other Domestic Animals
Smallholding & Farming
Wildlife
Trees & Woodland Crafts
Forestry
Orchards & Fruit Growing
Community
Building & Construction
Alternative Energy
Urban Issues
Transport
Money & the Economy
Trade Skills
Sustainabilty
Radical Thinking
Managing for Change

To obtain a FREE mail order catalogue send a large s.a.e. or contact us at the address below:

eco-logic books
10 -12 Picton Street, Bristol BS6 5QA, England
Telephone: 0117 942 0165   Fax: 0117 942 0164
email: books@eco-logic.demon.co.uk

Back garden seed saving